The Twelve Week Miracle

Changing Your World - not THE world - by

Changing Your Mind ... one step at a time

Anna and Philip J Bradbury

హఁఁ ఁఁఁ

Published by   The Write Site,
              Brisbane, Australia

Copyright 2019 © Anna and Philip J Bradbury

Anna and Philip J Bradbury have asserted their right under the Copyright, Designs and Patents Act 1988 to be identified as the authors.

ISBN- 978-0-9954398-2-5

All rights reserved. No part of this publication may be reproduced or transmitted in any form or by any means, electronic or mechanical, including photocopying, recording or any information storage and retrieval system, without permission in writing from the publisher.

"*The Twelve Week Miracle* gives you the opportunity to create real and lasting change in your life in just twelve weeks! It is full of practical advice and a host of valuable tools and techniques for transforming the way you view yourself and your life. It also gives you a clear structure and focus to your spiritual journey in a way that is easy to do and is hugely beneficial for you and your thinking. In short, it sets you up for miracles!"

Sarah Alexander coaches and runs workshops based on A Course in Miracles. She is the author of *Spiritual Intelligence in Business: The Eight Pillars of 21st Century Business Success*. Her website is www.sarah-alexander.co.uk

༺༺༺ ༻༻༻

"I love the way you have taken the best of *A Course in Miracles* (and other self-development material) and presented it in a simple program that would benefit anyone willing to follow it faithfully. I laughed aloud at the description of the Christian message (*Finding What's Wrong*), so in line with my own thinking. You would enjoy my Bible classes that cover the development of those ridiculous stories. I love the Wigoot section, but I could not endorse some of the statements in Lie #2 - suggestion of slander?"

Rhonda Murray, Unity Church Minister, Australia

༺༺༺ ༻༻༻

"Spiritual ideas are only worth something if one applies them to practical situations in everyday life. If they remain merely theory and intellectual concepts, they are worthless. Though its ideas are intended to be practically applied to life, A Course in Miracles is particularly prone to this trap. Anna and Philip Bradbury's book provides just such practical, everyday applications that take the Course's ideas out of the intellect and into experience. With humour and simplicity, they offer a 12-Week course that really can be a *new beginning*."

Ian Patrick was the Director of Miracle Network and is an ACIM course facilitator. Website at www.miracles.org.uk

"I am most impressed with *The Twelve Week Miracle* course. It gently nudges you and shows you, in twelve steps, how to stop being you own worst enemy and start being your own best friend. Its simplicity and ease of use is testimony to the vast knowledge, wisdom and expertise that Anna and Philip have to offer. Drink deeply as you work through *The Twelve Week Miracle*. It does what it says on the tin: bite size ideas that make you sit up and think. Stick with it, ponder it, learn your lessons well. Above all, be honest with yourself and you'll be amazed at how much you can change your world in just 12 steps."

Riana Avis is a Life Coach in Surrey, England. Her website is www.rianaavis.com/

"I think it is really excellent. I really like your message, I really like your quotations (so apt) and I really like your frequent acknowledgments of ACIM. I think your course is so great, so majestic, so potentially enormous, that I feel the cover and the title don't quite measure up to the content. I think specifically the word "Little" doesn't belong here. Congratulations!"

Michael Gould, Hastings, England and long-time student of *A Course in Miracles*.

[We changed the title of the book after Michael's comment!]

Contents

Finding You	7
Finding What's Wrong to Find What's Right	10
Lies, Addictions and WIGOOT	13
Lie #1 - Improving our outer world improves our inner world	13
Lie # 2 - The outer world is made up of levels	16
Addictions	19
Our Personal WIGOOT	21
A Course in Miracles	24
Miracles	25
Do not believe – just do	25
Nuts and Bolts	27
You Cannot Change The World	27
This course is not about changing the world.	27
This course is about changing your world.	27
Shopping List	27
The attitude you'll need	27
The people you'll need	28
The people you won't need – discernment required.	30
Daily Statement - DS	32
Weekly Theme - WT	32
Daily Journal - DJ	33
Week One	35
DS – "I will be still an instant and go home"	35
WT – Clutter Clearing	35
Exercises – Making a Space, Cadet	38
Week Two	41
DS - "My mind is still, peaceful and at one with the universe"	41
WT – Talk Talk In Your Head Head ... Mind Over Natter	41
Exercises – The Favourite Talk Talk In Your Head Head	46
Week Three	49
DS – "The world will not be the same without me"	49
WT – How Would The World Be Without Me?	49
Exercise – A World Without Me	50
Week Four	53
DS – "Every day, in every way, I'm getting better and better"	53
WT – Thought, Word And Deed	53

Exercise – Reviewing Previous Plans and Results	55
Week Five	57
DS – "This too will pass"	57
WT – Breakdowns And Breakthroughs	57
Exercises – Recreating Breakthroughs	60
Week Six	62
DS – "Feelings are not facts. I will go by what I know, not by how I feel."	62
WT – It's Only A Feeling	62
Exercises – Finding Facts And Deep Peace	66
Week Seven	68
DS - "I am never upset for the reasons I think"	68
WT – Anger And Depression	68
Exercises – Recovering the Connection	71
Week Eight	74
DS – "Let miracles replace all grievances"	74
WT – Regret And Guilt	75
Exercise – Dipping Under the Waves of Regret and Guilt	77
Week Nine	80
DS - "I can choose to see this differently."	80
WT – Events And Stories	80
Exercises – Recreating Your Stories	83
Week Ten	86
DS - "I am being the change I wish to see."	86
WT – It's All Smoke And Mirrors. Well, Mirrors Anyway	86
Exercise – Looking Into It	88
Week Eleven	89
DS – "All gifts I give others are my own."	89
WT – What Keeps You Going?	89
Exercise – What Are You Really Here For?	94
Week Twelve	96
DS - "Nothing is for nothing, everything counts. Does this action take me towards or away from my goal?"	96
WT – Acting As If	96
Exercise – You're Already There	99
A New Beginning	103
Letting Go	105
About the Authors	107
Books by Philip J Bradbury	108
Book by Anna Bradbury	108

We hate to spoil the ending but the story of your life will turn out alright!

Finding You

If this book has found your eyes and your heart, it knows that:
- Your life is a mess,
- Your life is becoming a mess, or
- You want to stop your life becoming a mess.

It also knows that there's nothing wrong with you, despite your outer circumstances and despite what you think of yourself and what you've done. You are a perfectly functioning person with intelligence, emotional maturity and a caring for yourself and others.

If things are not working out as you'd planned, there are two possibilities:
- Your plan was wrong and/or
- You're trying to achieve it in the wrong way – the way you've been taught by those in your world.

You see, if you pull back the happy face of every human being, no matter how smart, wealthy, healthy and successful they seem to be, there's sadness, anger and guilt behind every mask. We were taught to cope in this world by other sad, angry and guilt-ridden people. Despite all the gurus, psychologists, life coaches and others out there to help us get on with our precious lives, the world's still a sad, angry and guilt-ridden place – there's just as much war, abuse, rape, theft, depression, violence and despair as there ever was. And why? We've all been learning from dysfunctional people on how to dysfunction in a dysfunctional world. We keep doing the same old thing that people have been doing for thousands of years and hoping for a better result – the definition of insanity!

You're a perfect human being in an imperfect world, taught to operate imperfectly ... and your life is, well, imperfect? It must be if you've kept reading this far.

So, if the way we're all operating isn't working, what's next? Obviously, try another way. The chances are that that phrase – another way – has been haunting your waking and sleeping world. You've probably been looking for this other way for a long time. However, getting what we want, realising our dreams, is downright scary, for three reasons:

Firstly, we all feel we don't deserve to have our dreams realised, despite our most ardent protestations to the contrary.

Secondly, realised dreams mean that we have nothing to strive for and the worst thing to happen to any human is to take away the need for them to want more ... of anything!

The third problem with the other way is that it is another way. We don't know how long it took you to learn to tie your shoe laces, wash the dishes or wash yourself in the shower but, by now, you've got it down pat – you do these things every day, effortlessly, almost unconsciously. In fact, to explain how to do these things would be a challenge as we do them so automatically, so unconsciously, we're not aware of the process any more. Now, what we want you to do is learn to do these things the opposite way round. What your right hand did before, your left hand will now do and vice versa. Try it and see how difficult it is. Many years of practice are so ingrained that to undo that practice, that ingrained learning, is extremely difficult.

And so with every other task in our lives and, more importantly, everything else we think about in the world. This other way, this way to take you out of your mess, requires that you reverse a lifetime's thinking – thinking that's so ingrained that you probably don't even know what you think unless you're forced to stop and examine it.

Consider, also, the phrase, "Oh, it's only a thought." Only a thought? That's what we say and that means that we think that buildings, cars, careers, relationships, holidays, families and every other thing in this world is stronger or more important than a thought. Only a thought. Now consider what can be taken from you - buildings, cars, careers, relationships, holidays, families and every other thing, except your thoughts. Nothing can take your thoughts from you and it is, in fact, thoughts that created buildings, cars, careers, relationships, holidays, families and every other thing in this world.

Our thinking is crucial to our lives and responsible for the success of them, whatever success means to each of us.

This book, then, is set out in two sections:
1. What thinking and actions have got us into the mess we're in, and
2. What thinking and activities will take us out of our mess and into a life we both dream of and deserve.

Finding What's Wrong to Find What's Right

Let us examine what could possibly be going wrong and this will give us a platform on which to disassemble the dysfunctional and dismal and to reassemble the potent and peaceful.

When all is said and done, much has been said and little done. The priests, parsons, rabbis, imams and prophets have spouted a million words but our lives remain as tragic, humorous, pointless, meaningful, sad, happy or hopeful as they've ever been since we dragged ourselves from the alphabet soup or whatever it was that we dragged ourselves from.

People believe that a woman had sex with a ghost, gave birth to a wee chap who went on to be murdered so we wouldn't go to hell. Despite believing that this peaceful chap's murder has taken our sins from us, people also don't believe in him for they constantly fear the wrath of a loving God who could cast us into the oblivion of everlasting hell or damnation. There would be nothing to fear if that chap's murder really did expunge our sins and save us from hell.

Many people think like this:

God so loved his son that he had him killed – brutally and painfully for all the world to see. He so loves us that he brings us into the world in pain and, from that painful moment, abiding peace and happiness eludes us. The world he brings us into is filled with wretched sadness – wars, hunger, abuse, loss, disease, betrayal and drudgery. In brief moments we hit upon happiness or contentment but these moments never last. We fall in love but the bliss of the honeymoon is soon over. We win acclaim but the glory of it soon fades into the dust. We achieve riches but it's not long before we feel dissatisfied and want more. Our times of orgasms and triumphs are nothing as compared to our times of daily mundanity and struggle.

We spend our lives collecting strips of paper and metal disks and, because of the desperate love we have for them, we continually fear that there won't be enough and/or that they'll be taken away. So we use up some of those strips of paper and metal disks, paying people to save us from the possibility of loss – insurance companies, security companies, superannuation and investment schemes, accountants and other advisors. And that's never enough for the fear of loss is ever-present in all things – loss of money, relationships, jobs, health, happiness, prestige, power and life. No matter what we do, it seems, our God does nothing to save us from all of these possibilities. It seems he doesn't care about our safety, happiness or lives any more than he cares about the death of a moth or the colour of the sea.

And it's this to which our loving and forgiving Father brings us! Praise be that he's not a vindictive or vicious God!

A Course in Miracles describes a Christian god: "Careless indeed of him (us) this mind (God) must be, as thoughtless of his peace and happiness as is the weather or the time of day. It loves him not but casts him as it will in any role that satisfies its dream. So little is his worth that he is but a dancing shadow, leaping up and down according to a senseless plot conceived within the idle dreaming of the world."[1]

Dan Brown's character in *The Lost Symbol*, Robert Langdon, explains to his students that "… on the pagan day of the sun god Ra, I kneel at the foot of an ancient instrument of torture and consume ritualistic symbols of blood and flesh." This, he explains, is taking the Christian communion.

Then take the belief in atheism which is that there was is nothing and nothing happened to nothing and then nothing magically exploded for no reason, creating everything and then a bunch of everything rearranged itself for no reason whatsoever into self-replicating bits which then turned into dinosaurs.

Belief in the insanity of any of these stories has confined millions to their own torture chambers as they live their lives in fear

---

1 ACIM, chapter 27, VII, paragraph 8

and a belief in the utter depravity of what we supposedly are.

Many of us, however, feel that this is not what a loving father would want for his children. Yet, when we question this and put forward a more hopeful and uplifting possibility, we're told that it's insanity and other big ecclesiastical words.

Those who wish for fear, insanity and self-hatred cannot, will not, be dissuaded from their choices and all that's left to ask ourselves is, "How's that working for you?" If your deepest knowing has a sense of abiding peace to hold to current thinking then we wish you well.

However, if no abiding peace exists in your heart for where and how your beliefs have brought you to, we would like to offer another way – a way that's working for millions of others like you and us.

You don't have to understand this other way. You don't have to accept this other way. In fact, you can actively resist or reject this other way. All you have to do – and doing is the important part here – is apply your little willingness to it, in your daily life, and watch the miracles emerge.

If you dare for something different, something better, join us in an interesting voyage of peace, power and possibilities.

Let us start with undoing some of the erroneous beliefs and then we'll move on to what's more real and sane.

Lies, Addictions and WIGOOT

This world – and our lives – is based on two self-evident lies:
  • Improving our outer world improves our inner world, and
  • The outer world is made up of levels.
Both of these things lead us to our addictions.

Lie #1 - Improving our outer world improves our inner world

How many people think that having a new car, new job, new lover or new place to live will make their life better? We've tried it. You've probably tried it. Everyone has tried it in one way or another.

And did it work?

No, it never works. It might have appeared to have worked. You leap into a new job, new relationship, new health regime and, for a while, you're on the honeymoon – all roses and smiles and happy, happy days. Then you get home from the honeymoon, so to speak, and the ordinary, practical world sneaks up on you and, one by one, the rose petals die and the smiles fade.

There may be slightly different problems with your new job but the new problems are slightly more in number and slightly more stressful.

The neighbours at your new home are not so noisy but they're quietly stealing your mail.

Your new lover doesn't turn you down for sex but sure as heck has you working your butt off, earning brownie points for each sexual adventure.

Problems never go away when we only change our outer world. They seem to go away for a while but, soon, they sneak back in. In fact, as most of us have experienced, a new anything – to get away from the problems in the old anything – will soon bring you more problems than you've ever had before.

These problems are such sneaky chaps. Firstly, they disappear while the roses bloom and smiles shine. Then, as each petal dies they come back. And, sneaky little sods that they are, they pretend to come back in a different form and so we tell ourselves that we've escaped the previous problems. Then, one dark and chilly night, we have a little aha! moment. Those thieving neighbours are more abusive and disruptive than the previous (noisy) ones. It's a sad little moment for we realise that our problems are not only more in intensity and stress than the old ones, but they are the same dang problems as the old ones – just pretending to be different.

Your new lover doesn't insult you to your face (as your previous one did) but does it behind your back.

Your new boss isn't rude and demanding (as your previous one was) but polite and twice as demanding.

The new school for your children isn't openly racist (as the previous one was) but, though your son is now encouraged at gymnastics, he just doesn't seem to make the school team, despite his obvious talent.

The process, it seems, is that our problems treat us as a bit of a game, a simple dolt to have fun with. We think we're ever so clever and we always, always lose the game. Problems are unbeatable and they know it – they sit back and have a rest while we're in change-over mode, while we're on the honeymoon. Then, one day when we're lying back studying the insides of our eyelids and wondering if the roses were fake or the smiles were grimaces, our pet problems sneak back in with sinister laughs and evil aforethought, disguised as strangers and bop us over the head.

It's called an aha! moment. It can send us into a spin – anger and/or depression resulting.

So, whatever it was that brought on these more beastly problems with gnashing teeth and sharpened claws, we change again: another new lover, another new job, another new diet. And so these darker, sharper problems disappear for a moment and, just like before, return much bigger than before, fertilised, apparently, by our wonderful new situation.

Another aha! moment. Another bout of anger and/or depression. More confusion. More lashing out at an unfair world. More victim-hood. More "Why me?" More of everything you're ever experienced before.

Some people never stop to question themselves. Some people never want to learn and so they go through relationship after relationship, job after job, diet after diet.

How do we know this? We've done it all. At one point, Philip's first wife kindly reminded him that he had had eleven jobs in the previous ten years. That trend continued for another twenty five years. It was exciting and he met fascinating people and had amazing experiences – people and experiences that wouldn't have happened if he'd stayed in the one job. And, yes, there were many relationships and three marriages and, for the previous fifteen years he had lived nowhere for more than two years.

He knows about change. He knows how to drag problems behind him and how to fertilize them into massive and threatening triffids.

Then, surprise, surprise! He met Anna who made him her third husband and has done change upon change herself – change jobs, change homes, change men, change countries, change, change, change. We attracted to each other what we were – Change Masters and Problem Growers!

Of course, our fascinatingly varied lives were the envy of friends. Yes, it was exciting and fun and we definitely experienced all that life had to offer. On one level, we easily pretended that it's all hoopla and fun. However, it was also damned hard work and stressful, sometimes. For example, our finances were a mess – we owned nothing but a car, two computers, some furniture and clothes and we often didn't know where our next pound or dollar was coming from.

Philip had terrible trouble finding consistent work (and income) in England and so we decided to return to Australia … and then smiled knowingly at each other. Another change in the outer circumstances but, really, no change in anything at all.

We decided to try something new – change the inner and let the outer take care of itself.

Maybe parts or all of this story relates to you. Maybe it's why you're reading these words right now ... yet another change, yet another aha! moment, yet another bout of the same old problems, yet another dive into victim-hood and confusion, yet another binge of moaning at an unfair world. If this is where you are, right now, congratulations! You're on the road to real, abiding and uplifting change. If you're reading these words you've probably realised your old patterns haven't been working and you're questioning yourself. You may not know the answers. You may be beating yourself up mercilessly. You may be angry. You may be depressed. You may be confused. However, what you are also doing is stopping yourself, interrupting an old pattern, seeing the insanity of past actions and, finally, looking for new ways to find abiding peace of mind and all the good things we're all looking for – abundance of relationships, meaning, joy and a sense of being loving and loved.

You see, the evidence doesn't lie and, while we've all pretended that our frenetic and stressful lives are fun and/or normal, the evidence is that all is not as we want it. The evidence is also that what didn't work in the past won't work in the future and that it's insanity to try any of it again.

You're ready to learn. You're ready for honesty. You're ready for a change in the way of creating change. We hope you enjoy a whole new journey ... from the inside out this time.

Lie # 2 - The outer world is made up of levels

In the world of God we were part of the oneness. Without bodies we perceived and created our world by a simple and deep knowing. Then, being part of the magnificent oneness, we became dissatisfied. Though we were magnificent we were not special, different or unique from any other. Our desire for specialness created the world we know, whatever that is for each of us. We are different from you and you are different from every other creature in this world of separation. For, to be different is to be separate – separate from God and separate from each other.

And so our perennial conflict arises:

We spend our lives trying to join with others, attempting to make happy families, lifelong friendships, loving spouses, supportive colleagues and close communities. Then, at the same time, we try to separate from everyone and to stand out as special and unique from the crowd.

We see this conflict clearly in teenagers who assert that they want to be different and to challenge current values ... yet they wouldn't dare dress differently from their friends!

So we want to be different and we want to be the same and there is no way of reconciling this conflict.

In order to create the illusion of difference and uniqueness, we have set up a system of levels and of judgement, a way to make this black and that white, this up and that down, this right and that wrong, this better and that worse.

In this world of separation we have created bodies and organs for discerning and defining our world. Because these organs – eyes, ears, hands, noses, tongues – are on the outside, they can only discern the outer world, the world of shapes, colours, textures, smells and so on. These outer organs cannot detect or know of that larger, magnificent world from which we came and constantly wish to return to. We do detect snatches of that larger, more potent world in flashes of inspiration, fleeting dreams and inspirational moments but, by and large, our existence is rooted in the smaller, tangible world of form. It is upon tangible form that we base our judgements of our specialness, or otherwise: Is my car faster than yours? Is my house grander than yours? Is my income bigger than yours? Is my partner better looking than yours? Do more people like you or me? Is my body contoured better than yours? Are my children better behaved or educated than yours?

Each of us has, then, set up a series of levels of existence, based on outer form.

- Some of us say that eating meat is better than not eating meat. Others say the opposite.
- Some of us say that the bigger our car, the better we are. Others say the opposite.
- Some of us say that men should dominate women. Others say they shouldn't.
- Some of us say that being fat is a sign of power – it's good. Others say it's a sign of weakness – it's bad.

- Some say that thinking about adultery is the same as committing it. Others say that thinking about it is natural (good) and that committing it is immoral (bad).
- Some say that a smoking addiction is worse than a masturbation addiction as it affects many other people. Others say masturbation is worse as it's immoral.
- Some say that waging war and killing thousands of people you don't know is good. Others say it's bad.

These levels of existence – what's bad and good, what's better and worse – vary between us all and also vary over our lifetimes. In our 20s we may think that it's important to make money and families while in our 60s we may think it's important to make friends and peace with God.

Oh, how fickle we are and we don't even realise it!

Rupert Murdoch values his addiction to power over his personal happiness.

Amy Winehouse valued her addiction to alcohol over her life.

Tony Blair valued his need for money and fame over honesty.

Philip valued his sex and nicotine addiction over honesty and personal integrity, for many years.

Anna valued her need for alcohol, nicotine and control over peace, for many years.

Rupert Murdoch, Amy Winehouse, Tony Blair, Philip and Anna (in another life!) saw our choices as right and appropriate for the time we held those values. Many, many people hold the addiction to power and/or alcohol above all other values. Many, many people disagree and put both of these at the bottom level of their values.

Many, many people hold to their hierarchy of values all their lives. Caryl Chesman, Nelson Mandela and Mahatma Gandhi held to their principles (levels of existence), despite great pressure from others to change them. Many, many people like Elton John, Meat Loaf and us decided to let our addictions go (to change our values) to the bottom level of our values, prompted not from outside but by the inner need to feel more whole and free.

And so we judge, in this moment, that this is good and that is bad and, in another moment we take an opposite view. These fickle judgements may have something to do with our upbringing. Philip's great grandfather was an alcoholic and, because of that, his grandfather never drank alcohol.

Philip was molested by an uncle when he was five and raped by an older boy when in his early teens but he have never had a problem with others practising homosexuality. He does, however, have a problem with people abusing their powers over others. Out of those traumatic situations, the sexuality aspect had less impact than the hatred of being controlled by another. That was his choice, at some level.

We all make choices based on our personal view. Rupert Murdoch's son, David, is carrying on his father's tradition of power being more important than honesty. Meanwhile, many people reject their parents' ideas and preferences.

We will delve more into the influences of our upbringings later but, just for now, let us recognise that the values (levels) we hold to right now are downright unacceptable to someone else. And, further, they will likely change in the future, for us.

Addictions

We retreat into unhealthy or addictive behaviour to dull the consistent thudding of that remorseless despair and guilt in our lives. Not just some people. Everyone has some sort of addictive behaviour. It's the same despair and guilt that we all share, we all feel, and yet, in our supreme inventiveness, we have an endless array of ways out of (so we think) the swamp of our minds' self-created fear. We have so many choices; we can turn to alcohol, drugs, nicotine, sex, controlling, moving house, changing jobs, changing religions, changing relationships, gardening, television, computer games, work, perfectionism, procrastination, sport, talking-and-not-doing, reading-and-not-doing, finding cures for our addictions and on and on the brilliance of our ingenuity goes.

An addiction is anything we use to take our attention away from our perceived problems. An addiction stops us facing and dealing with the upsetting issues in our lives. Most of our addictions are healthy and it's only when we use them for avoidance that they become addictive. It's only when we cannot live our lives without them that they become addictions.

Many people enjoy a social drink from time to time. It's only when that "social drink" becomes a compulsion, when it begins to impact on our relationships, finances, careers and/or sense of self, that it becomes an addiction.

Masturbation is a natural act but when it becomes compulsive and when it undermines our relationships, career and/or finance, does it become an addiction.

Being proactive is seen as healthy. However, when that then grows into an overwhelming need to control circumstances and people, it becomes an addiction.

There's a fine line, a gossamer thread, between healthy and addictive behaviour. Because of that, it's difficult to see our healthy behaviour morphing into unhealthy behaviour.

Scientists tell us that if they place a frog into hot water it will immediately leap out. However, if they place a frog in cold water and gradually heat it up, the frog will remain in the water till it's boiled alive[2].

Like the frog, we can easily see unhealthy behaviour in others and we stay away (leap out) from them. However, when our healthy behaviour slowly morphs into unhealthy behaviour, into an addiction, we don't seem to notice. We stay in it, allowing it to kill our spirit and ruin our lives … until we decide we've had enough. We can all bury our heads in the sand but, eventually, the sand stops being a protection and threatens to suffocate us. The point at which we say, "Enough!" is often some trauma like divorce, redundancy, serious illness, heartbreaking loss or financial ruin. We scream at the universe in a silent and pitiful voice, "Enough!" We cry out that there must be another way. If that silent and pitiful scream of "Enough!" is sincere and determined enough, it will bring you what you need to find another way. This book is one of those things your Enough! has brought you. Do not be surprised if other guides – people, events, movies, books, overheard conversations, chance meetings and the like – come to you in quiet, welcome and unexpected ways.

Right now, we'll look at what is holding us to a particular world view, a behavioural thought choice for our lives … or what drives us into any and all addictions … our WIGOOT.

---

2 We have since found that frogs aren't that stupid and that the scientists lied. It is, however, a good story!

Our Personal WIGOOT

Every single thing we think, say and do is driven or inspired by what we perceive we'll get out of it. We don't consciously think, "What I'll Get Out Of This," but that's the basis on which we run our lives – WIGOOT.

We may perceive that Imelda Marcos, who owned 2,700 pairs of shoes, is quite illogical in buying yet another pair of shoes she'll never wear. However, to her, the decision is quite logical, based on her WIGOOT. Maybe there's an emptiness she thinks she can fill with another pair of shoes. Maybe she wants to break the world record for shoe ownership. We don't know. She may not know but her conscious or unconscious WIGOOT makes her do these things and nothing can stop her, unless she changes her WIGOOT.

We may think Richard III was insane, waging war to control yet more territory when he already controlled most of Europe. To him, however, his actions were quite normal and acceptable and, if we were able to discover his WIGOOT we'd know what drove his need to kill thousands of people he didn't know (and many he did), to control yet another piece of dirt and thousands more people?

What someone gets out of living a homeless life, when there is money and shelter available, is beyond most of us but people do it. It may seem insane but we don't know their WIGOOT – perhaps they feel a sense of rebellion, perhaps there's a level of comfort in living "outside society", perhaps they want others to feel sympathy for them, perhaps they want to feel self-pity, perhaps they don't want to work or to have the perceived stresses that others have. Perhaps, perhaps, perhaps. We don't know their WIGOOT – and they may not either – but it's powerful enough to drive them to do what they do, despite the bodily discomfort.

On the other hand, George Michael, with more homes (and private toilets) than most of us, was driven to let himself be caught doing embarrassing things in public toilets. We can only imagine what drove him to do that and, though he might not know himself, he could stop himself until he uncovered his WIGOOT and changed it.

Logic and sanity play no part in our life choices – they're driven by unrequited needs that sneak around in the hidden depths of our separate minds.

Nothing is ever not worth the Love

When sight was ever doomed
A life never bloomed

The void was never filled
With but guilt that ever killed

A joy that slowly died
And a peace that would hide

'Tis no pain came more fraught
When attack's net was caught

Though the light could not fade
It seemed guilt it forbade

Taken no more but trust
A waking eye under dust

Does see the spark though dim
Drawn forth a thought but slim

A hope, a dream, a long ago
Does memory unearth a tiny glow

A promise, a shimmer, a beam
A hidden thought, a dream
Nothing stops a seed when fed
Though the dark earth looks dead

A light not yet seen
Draws it forth, ever keen

Willing sprout with gentle ease
Cannot stop if it please

It knows the light, yet unseen
Does nourish with softest gleam

Once the soil, it breaks to light
There's nothing left to fight

And up it grows, tendrils reach
Sun and water its growth to teach

A mighty seed we all look out
Immersed in now't but doubt

A heavy world might give us lack
And thoughts of sin do bend our back

We can't stop sprouting, tiny smiles
Thought filth of malice our heart defiles

A tiny glimpse, a secret memory
Does move us up to see more, aye

Through slugs and snails and slush we creep
Knowing our way to a life more deep

Unstoppable, indefensible, pulled from above
And though it don't rhyme
Nothing is ever not worth the Love

A Course in Miracles

A Course in Miracles (ACIM) is a self-study, psycho-spiritual course in forgiveness. As Gerald Jampolsky says in his book, *Love Is Letting Go Of Fear*, "Forgiveness does not mean condoning or agreeing with a horrendous act. It is a decision to no longer attack one's self. Forgiveness is, quite simply, the decision not to suffer. To forgive is to make the decision to be happy, to let go of judgements, to stop hurting others and ourselves and to stop recycling anger and fear. Forgiveness is the bridge to compassion, to inner peace and to a peaceful world."

The Course uses Christian terminology like *God, Holy Spirit* and *Christ* but with slightly different meanings from the many meanings in the many different Christian sects. However, the Course is not religious and it is not a religion. Since its transcribing in 1973, over two million copies of the book have been sold and, included in the millions who follow the Course are Catholic priests, Jewish rabbis, Buddhists, Hindus and people from every religion, creed, nationality and age. There is no leader, no rituals and no prescriptions on what to wear, eat, work at or where or how to live.

What the Course does ask of us is a little willingness and it tells us that, to follow it, it is both simple and difficult.

What it asks us to do – to change our minds, to change the way we think about others and our world and to forgive ourselves – is simple. It can be done by young and old, rich and poor, intelligent and ignorant and it can be done anywhere and at any time.

The difficult part is in doing this simple thing every day, every minute, of our lives. The Course tells us that we do not forget to undertake the diligent practice. We don't practice it diligently because we believe we don't deserve the peace, power and joy that come from constant practice.

Miracles

It's called *A Course in Miracles* and it's, therefore, helpful to know what a miracle is. The Course's definition of a miracle is not walking on water, turning water into wine or feeding 5,000 people with a fish and some bread. Miracles are not incredible physical feats; they are incredible mental feats. A miracle is a change of mind, an inner shift in perception. The Course says that, "the most sacred place on Earth is where an ancient hatred has been replaced by a present love." The most ancient and abiding hatred we all have is for ourselves. The greatest miracle, then, is to be able to turn the disappointment, hatred and guilt for ourselves into that which reflects what we truly are – amazing, powerful and lovable sons and daughters of a loving God.

When we're able to access, believe in and live that self-love, our lives change, our world changes and we're no longer hampered by our self-defeating behaviour. That is a miracle and that's what this course is about – you moving from guilt to love and experiencing your God-given talents and knowingness, every single day!

Do not believe – just do

We (Anna and Philip) have been studying this course since 2005 and we are not perfect students. The Course tells us, "Remember only this; you need not believe the ideas, you need not accept them and you need not even welcome them. Some of them you may actively resist. None of this will matter or decrease their efficacy. But do not allow yourself to make exceptions in applying the ideas the workbook contains and, whatever your reactions to the ideas may be, use them. Nothing more than this is required." And so, like good students, we do not always believe, accept or welcome the ideas and many times we actively resisted them. We do, however, apply the ideas with "a little willingness" (when we remember) and, as time goes on, we find we "remember" more and more. What we can say is that the Course is transforming our lives and it is transforming our relationship. Without it we would not be together (happily together) and we both shudder to think where we'd be – physically, financially and emotionally – if we hadn't applied a little willingness.

They say that the truth will set you free but it may annoy the heck out of you in the meantime. ACIM will probably annoy the heck out of you and we know of several people who can vouch for this, including us. We have a friend, John, in England, who has destroyed two copies of the Course book. One he threw out the window of his apartment and the other he studiously ripped up, one by one, every one of the 1,122 pages! He got mad but the Course got even. It wasn't long before, each time, that the Course called him back and he bought yet another book. Some time ago he told us that he used to be filled with anger and that, now, he finds it impossible to hold a negative thought in his mind for more than a second.

The Course tells us, time and time again, that what's in our minds is what's in our world. So, like John, the benefits of the Course start in the mind and we soon find them spilling over into our relationships, friendships, careers, finances and all other aspects of our lives. This course is a course in mind-training and it's a practical course that can be applied in every practical and emotional aspect of our lives.

The *ACIM* book can be purchased in many book stores, from www.amazon.com and from the Foundation for Inner Peace (www.acim.org).

We know the Course works and this is what our 12-Week course is based on. Let's get started …

Nuts and Bolts

You Cannot Change The World

This course is not about changing the world.

This course is about changing your world.

Shopping List

The attitude you'll need

All that is required is a little willingness – just do the exercises. You may resist, from time to time, the ideas in this course – just do the exercises. You may disbelieve the exercises in this course – just do the exercises and watch your life transform itself before your eyes!

The tools you'll need
1. A journal (maybe 2) into which you will write your daily exercises and observations,
2. A pen, obviously!

Go and get those two things right now. No excuses!

So, have you got your journal and pen? If so, your willingness is there too – you're on your way! If not, what's stopping you? Are you ...

Afraid of success?

Afraid of having no excuses to fail?

Afraid of standing out from the crowd?
Afraid of losing that which you do not want?

Now that you have your journal in front of you, open, describe your perfect day - what would it look like?

Do it now. Why?

Simply this - you have not bumped into this course by accident. You're here because, like so many other people, you want to change something in your life:

- Work
- Prosperity
- Relationships
- Health
- Self-image
- Sense of purpose
- Sense of achievement ...

... you can easily complete the list yourself.

So, why are we ordering you to do something you're resistant about? Easy - if you want a different result, you need to take different actions. If you want something, you need to DO something.

So, if you're resisting getting that piece of paper and a pen, ask yourself, "What am I resisting?" "Why am I resisting?"

Is it that:
- You don't know what your perfect day is?
- That perfect day is so far from what you're currently experiencing that it brings a lump to your throat?
- You feel there's no point as your life won't change anyway, so why bother trying?
- You can't be bothered?

There is never a good reason for holding yourself back – this world needs you and you'll only grow old and bitter if you do. Do something, each day, to be proud of ... today it's writing about your perfect day.

The people you'll need

... if the years have taught me anything it is that no man or nation can do any effective work in the world alone. It is only by working together for a common cause that civilization be carried forward.
Louise Carnegie, wife of Andrew Carnegie

No one ever conquered their world alone – we all need others and never more so when we're infected by the bug of change. So, it might seem to be safer to do this course alone but it's not. It may seem to feel safer if no one's looking in your dirty laundry basket, seeing:
1. What mental filth you've accumulated,
2. What mistakes you've made,
3. What embarrassments you've caused yourself, and
4. What you've failed to live up to, to date.

It might seem safer to avoid scrutiny when no one can see:
1. When you're having a bad day,
2. When you fail to turn up at the course every now and then,
3. When you make a promise to yourself and fail to deliver, and/or
4. When you hit a hard patch and can't seem to go on.

You know what? It's a darned sight harder on your own. Do you know why? Because you're the harshest, most unrelenting critic of yourself and no one – absolutely no one in this world – will get down on your perceived faults like you do. So, the benefits of having a friend doing the course along with you are:

- There is someone to moderate the hard time you're giving yourself – someone to smite you (with a feather) on the head when you start getting too hard on yourself,
- There is someone else who can see the beauty and brilliance of you when you forget,
- There is someone to bounce ideas around with,
- There is someone who may see other aspects and perspectives that you cannot,
- There is someone to share the success moments with,
- There is someone to share the scary bits with,
- There is someone who understands the new language you're developing,
- There is someone who understands the changes that are going

on within you,
- There is someone to share the journey with, and
- There is someone with whom you'll develop a truly close and lasting relationship with through doing this course together.

So, if you want to enhance your relationship with your spouse/partner or a close friend, ask them to join you – do this epic journey together!

The people you won't need – discernment required.

This is not a 12-Week program but if you were doing one, they would tell you not to tell anyone that you're doing it till you're at least half-way through the 12 steps. Good advice.

We've said that it's great to do with a friend, and it is. However be discerning about who you do this with and who you tell. We do not want anyone to discourage you from doing what you feel is very right for you, especially at the start when you're taking your first small steps. In fact, you probably won't need to tell anyone about your challenge of change because, if you're doing it by yourself or with a friend, privately, people will soon notice something about you anyway. Some may even say to you that they've noticed a change, that they can't quite work out what it is but, whatever it is, you're looking happier, more peaceful and/or certain of yourself. If they ask you what you've been up to, be open and tell them. That's better than becoming an overbearing evangelist, trying to force your new "religion" down peoples' throats. They'll not thank you for that. Best to wait for them to create the opportunity.

Ponder this:

The longer you've known someone, the more they're used to how you are ... and the more resistant they may be to any changes you want to make, because:

1. They like you how you are and don't want to see you change. Even if you're not planning any external changes – in your job, business, relationships or location – and simply want to feel better about yourself, more peaceful, fulfilled and happy, any change could challenge them. They could be jealous of seeing you have something they want.

2. Your commitment to change means they could be confronted

with their own unfulfilled desires for change. Your self-commitment may remind them of their own lack of commitment to themselves - they haven't got it and they're doing nothing about getting it, whatever *it* is.

3. If you change, you might seek different company/interests – they may fear losing you.

Those three above fears can be disguised as love and concern. Witness the friends of a dieter who say, "Oh, another muffin won't matter!" Or a recovering alcoholic who is badgered into having "just another little drink". Or the 'encouraging' parent who says, "Yes, what a lovely idea, dear, but are you sure you should give up your accounting career?"

They say their concern is all for you but it's actually about them.

So, before you shout your plans from the rooftops, decide very clearly – very clearly indeed – what kind of support you want. This course is for you and you need to become selfish about that – you can't run on empty and, if you're not full, you'll have nothing to give to others. Don't let anyone pull you back from your commitment to growth and fulfilment – no one is served by that. If you're undecided about someone, they're probably not going to help push you to where you want to go.

You're looking for pushers and not pullers. You'll know a pusher as your gut instinct, your intuition, will tell you clearly that they'll help. When you feel that big "YES" about someone, don't be afraid to ask for help and support – their gift is in helping someone else.

So, how do you do this course? What do you do each day?

The course is called *The 12-Week Miracle* so it is done in 12 steps. Now, those steps can be any length of time you like; rather like *A Course in Miracles* that is, supposedly, a one-year course. However, Anna and Philip (and millions of others) have been doing that one-year course for many, many years!

Most people have been doing this 12-Week course over 12 weeks and so that's how we've set it up here.

There are three aspects to each step, to each week:
1. Daily Statement
2. Weekly Exercises/Themes
3. Daily Journals

Daily Statement - DS

Each week you will have a daily statement – or affirmation – to say to yourself. If you like them, you can continue beyond the week. *A Course in Miracles*, which also has daily affirmations, tells us that we do not forget to say them – we choose, at an unconscious level, not to say them as we believe we don't deserve the benefits they bring. So, not only do the daily affirmations bring you their benefits, they also serve to remind you what you think you deserve.

So, how do you do them? Simply choose/create 3-5 minutes at the beginning and end of each day – a quiet and uninterrupted time. The best is before you get out of bed in the morning and just before going to sleep. Simply be present with yourself, relaxed with eyes closed. Start saying the statement for the week to yourself, twice a day.

Sound simple? What you may find is that your mind wanders to the past or the future – reliving old good or bad experiences, remembering people, events and feelings, thinking and dreaming about the future and all the people, events and feelings you might imagine you'll meet when you get there. When you notice your mind wandering away from the present, the now and your Daily Statement, simply bring your mind back and start saying the statement to yourself again.

Be kind to yourself for everyone's mind wanders off to the past and future, trying to escape NOW. Just bring your thoughts back to now, to the Daily Statement, and do it again and again each time your mind wanders off. With gentle diligence, twice a day, your mind will wander less and less. The less it wanders, the clearer your thoughts will be during the day.

Be kind. Be persistent.

Weekly Theme - WT

There will be some reading each week and that will be the theme of the week, around which your daily exercises are based. Do not feel constrained by this – if you find exercises from previous weeks' to be particularly helpful, continue doing them, while still doing the current week's exercises.

Daily Journal - DJ

Each day, throughout the whole course, write a daily journal – your experiences, ideas, feelings, thoughts, successes, blockages and general ruminations on the day just experienced. Most people find it essential to choose a particular time of day that they can have an uninterrupted half-hour, and stick to that time – doing their journal at the same time each day. Most people grow to love that special time with their journal and themselves.

Remember, no one is ever going to read your journal so the language, grammar and look of it doesn't matter. It's about getting what's in your head out of it and down on paper. This has several benefits:

1. By getting everything out of your head and on to paper, you create a space for clearer thinking – there will be more room in your mind for BFI[3]s about yourself and others.
2. Constantly looking forward to where you want to be can be depressing for we're never totally happy about where we are – that's why you chose to do this course! However, after some time of journalling, you can look back on where you were and heave a sigh of relief and/or have a laugh as you realise you have, indeed, been making progress.
3. Some people treat themselves to a regular massage or pedicure – this is a way of pampering or valuing themselves. Doing your daily journal is a way of valuing, or pampering, your mind and your future. You are obviously worth the (say) 30 minutes a day it takes to write your journal – you're actually worth all 24 hours a day of your time but the outside world does intervene at times! This is your time to say, "No, I am taking this sacred time for my sacred journey as I am worth it." And you are.
4. There will be times when your dreams slip away from you or you forget or choose not to follow them, when the going gets too hard. Your journal will hold your dreams when they slip from you. It will be the friend who reminds you that you do, indeed, have dreams and that they are there, waiting for you to reactivate them.

---

3 BFI = *Blinding Flash of Insight*

5. If you're at all interested in writing as a career, you can use your daily journal as the basis for your autobiography or novel and make millions!
6. You might like to have two journals – one for your daily journal and one for your weekly exercises. Or, you might like have one journal and do your daily journals at the front and the exercises at the back. Or, you might like to do the daily journals and exercises after one another, chronologically. It's up to you.

Week One

Purpose: to become aware of where we focus our thoughts.

We must not, in trying to think about how we can make a big difference, ignore the small daily differences we can make which, over time, add up to big differences that we often cannot foresee.
~ Marian Wright Edelman

DS – "I will be still an instant and go home"

This statement is from *A Course In Miracles*. Simply say this to yourself, morning and evening, each day this week, per the instructions two pages back. Your "home" is any place you feel entirely safe – your first home, your mother's or father's arms, a beach, a favourite café, with a particular friend, your spiritual place, the God of your understanding. This is your home and, in your mind, you can be there whenever you still yourself.

Write the statement down and place it somewhere that you'll notice it often – in your diary, on your fridge, on your desk etc. As often as possible, simply say it to yourself. Also, when you are stressed, worried, stuck or frustrated, stop for a minute and say it quietly to yourself.

WT – Clutter Clearing

Start in a small space – where you are right now.
When Martin Luther King Junior started his mission, he had no intention of reforming the race relations problem in America.

Initially, he saw that his people were abused and frightened and so he resolved, in his little church with his little congregation, to help them to feel safe for half a day a week. That was all he could hope to do, he felt. So, on Sunday afternoons, he attempted to create a safe space for the few black people in his congregation – a safe space physically in the church and, by talking to them, to create for them a sense of empowerment within and a sense of hope for the future. By concentrating his love and energy into that small group, his reputation grew and more and more people came. He was soon being asked to talk in other churches and, by and by, he was talking to the whole nation ... by starting small.

Mother Theresa had no intention, at the start, of becoming world famous. She started by concentrating her love and energy on one small block of that massive city of Calcutta. By doing such an impressive job in that small space, more and more requests came. She started recruiting more nuns and training more volunteers and so her mission grew. Then, by popular demand, as they say, she was asked to set up more missions in different places and, eventually she was talking at the United Nations and has become a household name and will be remembered for centuries ... by starting small.

Just take the first step. You don't need to see the whole staircase. Just take the first step. ~ Martin Luther King Jnr.

Both of them started small and finished big – that's what we want for you.

Start in an even smaller space – your mind.
After training in meditation for six years, Buddha realised he was close to attaining full enlightenment. Sitting under the Bodhi tree, he vowed not to rise from meditation until he had attained perfect enlightenment. After many tests and worldly temptations for his mind, over seven weeks, he attained enlightenment. In a similar way, Jesus trained for many years and then went into the desert for forty days and nights. Like the Buddha, his mind was tortured by fearsome and enticing worldly temptations, which he rose above. For both men, it was only after observing and rejecting the insanity of the world that they were able to clear their minds enough to see

a greater reality of themselves and the world.

Similarly, Mother Theresa and Martin Luther King Jnr., as a nun and pastor, started out in their worldly missions in much silent contemplation, releasing their fears and prejudices and clearing their minds of the clutter of the world. Their defenselessness and their fearlessness became their power for they had overcome the hardest tests – those of the mind. Anything "the world" threw at them was, therefore, insignificant.

Let's do what the experts do.

We can think of no better examples of long-lived fame and positive action than the Buddha and Jesus – still famous after 2,000 years! Mother Theresa and Martin Luther King Junior thought so too as they followed these examples. The time they spent in quiet contemplation of their own weaknesses, fears and prejudices was well spent. That time allowed them to change their minds about who they really were and what their passions were. Once the clutter of the world's insanity was cleared away, they were able to see, with great clarity, what was real and what was important for them.

This we wish for you.

What the above four people realised, as have so many other great people, is that the world is insane. There is no point in trying to understand it. People do stupid things in politics, sport, business, war, their communities, their families … every part of existence. There is no benefit in trying to understand it – if you try, it can drive you insane!

Start with yourself and stay with that until you understand who you really are ... that is a lifetime mission!

That self-understanding and self-respect (or self-confidence) will be the solid launch-pad from which you propel yourself into whatever area of life you choose – being a great dancer, leader, parent, friend or anything else. Also, with greater freedom from clutter and greater clarity, you will see, much more clearly, what your talents and passions are and what you're on earth for.

It all starts with a little stillness in the little space – your mind – and evolves into the big job – creating a life to be proud of … the big little job!

What you also know is that every human being is important, no matter how famous or admired they are. Every one of them makes a difference, whether they try to or not. Everyone is needed – otherwise they wouldn't be here.

You're here because you're needed, though it may not feel like it at times! You're here because of your precious gifts, whatever they are.

Part of our mission, on this course, is to unlock those precious gifts of yours and the other part of our mission is to help you start using them. Both parts of this mission are equally important and most of it depends on you. Sorry, but it mainly depends on you. We'll play our part and we know you will.

Exercises – Making a Space, Cadet

Your mission for this first week, should you choose to accept it (which you will as you definitely do want a more peaceful and abundant life!) is this:

Day One ... Observations on my mind's input

For each piece of communication you have during this day, mark the aspects of it for its negative and positive comments, in your journal.

For example, for the newspaper you normally read, count the negative articles (about bloodshed, crime, anger, loss, criticism) that make you angry, bitter or depressed. Then the positive articles (about great and positive human achievement) that make you smile or laugh or articles that bring tears to your eyes for their positive impact. Then put the number in each column.

Do the same for magazines and social media and so on.

At the top of the first page write today's date and the number "one" ... for exercise one!

Now, start a column down the left-hand side with the appropriate words and two narrower columns down the right-hand side:

Media/Conversation	Negative	Positive
Newspaper articles	e.g. 24	e.g. 8
Magazine articles	13	16
Facebook/other social media	3	26
Family conversations	91	7
Friends conversation	5	6
Work conversations	6	5
Television programmes	14	3

Etc	?	?
TOTAL	e.g. 161	e.g. 83

Rest of the week ... accentuate the positive

There are several things you can do during the week:

With your trusty journal to hand, ready for your written observations, notice which newspaper, magazine and television articles/programmes and conversations you are attracted to – are they negative ones (tragedy, hard luck stories, gossip, failure etc) or are they positive ones (happiness, upliftment, success, humour etc)? Make a note, also, of why you are attracted to them.

Eckhart Tolle talks about our pain bodies, which are unhappy minds which like to see unhappiness everywhere else – a truly active pain body will find bad in everything. Caroline Myss talks about our wounds and the fact that we attract people with similar wounds – we'll talk about this in week nine.

As well as the above, we suggest that you look for as many ways to release the negative and bring in the positive to your life.

Choose not to buy into the negatively competitive conversations, like "I sliced the end of my finger off ..." "Oh, I broke my arm last year ..." "Yea but I was hospitalized for a week last month ..." "But did you hear about that highway crash, last night, where 5 people were injured ..." "That's nothing, did you hear about that air accident where 129 people died ..." Without noticing it, we're drawn in and trying to compete for the worst story.

So, you might like to break the horror up by saying that you'd sat in the park at lunchtime, watching children on the swings and it had you feeling very light and happy, or something else to bring you back to a positive reality.

Choose not to buy into the terrible weather = terrible day type of conversation. When someone says it's a bad day, you can respectfully remind them that it's raining or windy or snowing or whatever, but you're having a good day.

Eleanor Roosevelt once said, "Great minds discuss ideas; average minds discuss events; small minds discuss people." Observe and note down what you and the people around you talk about and what's important to all of you.

Rest of the course
Start a media fast – during the rest of this course you may like to stop reading the newspaper, listening to the radio and watching the television. If you really must do any of them, choose to avoid the news and the weather and watch/listen to/read inspiring and happy programmes. You might even choose to listen to your favourite music or watch uplifting movies. You could even swap the times you used to watch the news and weather for time writing your daily journal. [Note: After you're done the media assessment exercise above!]

This week's exercises are focused on just observing where we focus our thoughts and what we fill our environment with. With a raised awareness, we can start to make more healthy choices about what we let at our senses.

If you want to take this another step and actually start to extract some of the negative and disturbing thoughts you have, you might like to try the *Letting Go* exercise on page 105.

Week Two

Purpose: getting control of our thoughts.

DS - "My mind is still, peaceful and at one with the universe"

Our minds are full of chatter, full of thoughts, and it can be difficult to get them to stop for a little peace of no-mind. It is possible to have our racing mind still itself and it can take time to achieve that. However, a way to start is for you to direct your thoughts to where you want them to be, rather than have them in control. So, if the mind must think of something, have it focus on peace and stillness – the more you do this, the more you will have peace and stillness.

WT – Talk Talk In Your Head Head ... Mind Over Natter

To put the world in order, we must first put the nation in order; to put the nation in order, we must first put the family in order; to put the family in order, we must first cultivate our personal life; we must first set our hearts right. ~ Confucius

Having done the first week's exercises, you may have entered observations in your journal, like:
... this stuff seems so pointless, why should I bother?
... I feel quite silly doing this, is it worth it?
... I could be out there doing much more useful things with my time than these silly journalling exercises.

On and on your mind may be chattering at you, giving you all sorts of reasons not to make a change in your life ... and they're such logical reasons too! The Buddhists call this the monkey mind, imagining it as a mischievous monkey or a naughty child. You are the parent and you have the means to take back your power. Your power is in NOW.

Somewhere in the back of your thoughts is a still, small voice that assures you that this course is worthwhile. That still, small voice also tells you that those people who did the previous exercise, no matter how silly or pointless it seemed to them, experienced a shift, a change in their lives. Beside the annoyance that may accompany the exercises is a sense of peace, of rightness, and a knowing that if this process has benefited so many other people it will also have huge benefits for you. Which voice do you want to listen to?

One of the disadvantages of this talk talk is that the more we allow it, the more it talks. If we're worried about something, the talk talk starts thinking all sorts of awful scenarios, which makes us worry more, which accelerates the monkey mind's chatter, which makes us feel even worse ... and so our whole being is consumed by the horror of the situation we're imagining.

When we still our minds, we can return to a semblance of peace. Anna's technique is to ask light to surround the negative feeling inside – try that when you're upset and your mind's rushing around more franticly.

People ask how they can have peace of mind and the answer is that they cannot. The only thing that is peaceful is the state of no-mind, the mind that is without thoughts.

Ponder on this for a moment:

You are observing a crowd of people – what is that crowd? Is it a thing or a process? If half of the people leave, will there still be a crowd? If another half of that leave will it still be a crowd? If all leave, except one person, is it still a crowd? So what constitutes a crowd – 2, 3, 10, 20 people? And when all the people leave, where will the crowd go?

Obviously, the crowd went nowhere because it does not exist. It is not a thing, it is a process, made up of the gathering of a number of people.

So it is with our mind – it is like the crowd and only exists by virtue of the thoughts that flow through it. If we have no thoughts, where has our mind gone? The answer is that our mind has gone nowhere for it never existed in the first place – it was never a thing. Our mind is nothing but a collection of thoughts and when they go, it ceases to exist. Aha, peace at last!

Another way of explaining this is, as *A Course In Miracles* says, the ego always speaks first and always speaks loudest. When it finally stops its clatter and clamour, when we still ourselves enough to listen, that second, quiet voice may be heard. Few people hear it and fewer heed to its wisdom.

This quiet, gentle voice of knowing may be called the Voice for God, the Whisper of Angels, the Rhythm of the Universe , the Breath of Buddha, the Tongue of Allah and many other things. Every culture knows about this quiet wisdom and the few who heed it know of its power. That is one reason we asked you to try to eliminate the negative racket that blasts at us every day, from the media and outer sources, in Week One. When you stop that outer clamour and can get past the ego's constant talk talk, you will start to discern that deeper wisdom that whispers to your soul about what's real in this life and what's real about you. We want to help you access that ever-present knowledge for it is the only true guide to heed.

Until you hear the Voice for God (as we'll call it here) this ego talk talk will natter on in every moment of your life, whisper its demeaning and judgemental messages into your brain. When you're not aware of it, it runs your life, telling you silently that you're less than perfect and so is everyone else. Once you're aware of it, you can loosen its hold over you.

In so many ways that negative talk talk wheedles its way into your brain, down into your body and out into your life, spoiling chances and ruining dreams. This ego talk talk conspires to ruin each and every day, if we let it: we pull a muscle the day before the marathon we've trained for all year; we have a bad asthma attack just minutes before the final exam of our three-year degree; we lose our keys just before leaving for a holiday; we tuck our dress into our pantyhose just before the interview for our dream job; we break out in pimples just before our first big date; we burn the roast the first time we invite our boss for dinner and in every way and every day it finds imaginative ways to spoil our chances at life.

The talk talk in our heads is constantly telling you that someone else is going to stuff it up for you or that you aren't good enough or don't deserve to have your aspirations come true. If you're unsure about this, ponder for a moment ...

Think of the last time you went into a room you hadn't been in before – what conversation went on in your head?

- Don't like this carpet.
- What a silly painting.
- They must be wealthy here.
- What a dirty place.
- Love that window seat.
- What a nice view.
- What a stupid idea putting tartan and paisley together.
- Must cost a packet to heat this old place.

The talk talk is constantly burbling in judgmental tone about every little thing, comparing it with what you've got, with what you like and dislike and with what you've seen before. And, from the good/bad judgements of what you see, your talk talk creates a story about how good/bad, wealthy/poor, nice/nasty, beautiful/ugly, intelligent/stupid, local/foreign, kind/selfish etc. the owner of the room must be. And this whole talk talk conversation is before you have met the people you're judging! The summing up of someone you've never met only takes a fraction of a second.

Now that your talk talk has decided what the person's like, they appear. Even if the talk talk's initial judgement is totally wrong, it blunders on, unperturbed by failure, and now goes to work on the person before it:

- What a big nose.
- What nice legs.
- What kind eyes.
- How can anyone wear that tie with that shirt?
- Hmm, shorter than I thought.
- Hmm, shorter than me ... good!
- Looks foreign ... must be Swedish.
- Probably born into money.

And so the talk talk continues on its relentless and judgemental way.

While the constant noise of your talk talk continues to judge the outside world, it does that in terms of you. The essence of its constant harping is to judge everyone else and, from that, decide how good/bad, wealthy/poor, nice/nasty, beautiful/ugly, intelligent/stupid, local/foreign, kind/selfish, etc. you are. Sadly, 99% of the judgement of your talk talk is that you're not good enough in some way:

I'm too fat.
I'm too skinny.
I'm too unfit.
I'm too ugly.
I'm too stupid.
I have nothing useful to say.
I don't deserve this.
I always stuff things up.
I don't fit in.
I'm too poor.
I'm too old.

With that conversation constantly yapping in your head, is it any wonder that you choose to pass up opportunities you'd love to pursue – people you'd love to meet, jobs you'd love to apply for, holidays you'd love to have, hobbies you'd love to do, businesses you'd love to start, assets you'd love to own and other things you'd love to do? And, not only do you have conversations going on in your head (even in your sleep, sometimes!), your body has similar "conversations" by reacting in ways that stop you doing what you'd love to do ... your body obeys your mind.

Example
Mary told us how she had twice enrolled at university, in her native Scotland, to complete a fine arts degree. Each time, as she was about to start the study, she found herself pregnant. She realised that the timing of her pregnancies meant that she never quite started her dream career. Once she had a degree, she now realised, others would then have expected her to do something with it and, with all that expectation, there was the possibility of public failure. So, in unconscious choosing, she had created "pregnant pauses" to her dreams. Eventually, she had had enough. Marriage was unfulfilling, motherhood was boring, she was overweight and nobody wanted

her artwork. In one year she transformed herself and her first step was to say, "I've had enough! I want my life back! NOW!" She took charge of her life, set the ego talk talk aside and began listening to the real voice inside. She lost the five stone, regained the passionate and fulfilling relationship with her husband, found four beautiful and fun-filled friends in her children, had started painting again and art dealers had started knocking on her door, asking her to name her price.

So how do we release ourselves from those conversations, from that talk talk that we seem to be stuck with? No, you do not need to go into deep analysis, prolonged counselling and years of painful therapy. The technique is painless, free, can be done in the comfort of your home or anywhere else and only needs the intervention of you – no one else. Simply accept that you have a favourite talk talk conversation with yourself and, in that knowing, it will make itself known to you. When you are aware of it, simply acknowledge it for it's help in getting you out of "trouble" in the past, thank it and allow it to move on. And move on it will if you are passionate and sincere about following your passions.

Exercises – The Favourite Talk Talk In Your Head Head

Day One ...

The exercise here is to simply stop whatever you're doing and listen …no, put that pen down, don't make a coffee, don't answer the phone, don't have a stretch, don't go to the toilet, don't go for a walk and don't keep reading. If you're tempted to do anything but be still, observe very carefully what you're planning to do and know that that could be a part of your talk talk speaking.

- If you want to keep reading, ignoring problems could be your technique.
- If you want to go to the toilet, walking away from things could be your technique.
- If you want to make a coffee, eating could be a part of your technique.
- If you want to call someone, passing the buck could be your technique.

1. Observe

Firstly, take three to five minutes to observe the urges that come from your talk talk and know that it cannot stay still and quiet for long. Don't fight the urge – simply acknowledge it. It might immediately disappear and when you are still and quiet, you might start to hear the conversation in your head – the "I'm not good enough" conversation. Try to distinguish why you're not good enough and when you've made that distinction, simply acknowledge and give thanks.

2. Write
When you hear that talk talk voice, write it down – there is nothing it hates more than being noticed. Write it down as if you were taking dictation – someone in your head is speaking and you're its secretary. Simply write, don't analyse any of it, yet.

For the rest of the week ...

3. Share with friends and release
If you really want to have a good laugh, invite several friends around and do the exercise together. Once you've each found your favourite talk talk conversation, introduce yourself to each other with your name and your conversation. Say, "Hello, I'm Mary and I'm too fat," or "Hello, I'm Frank and I'm too stupid," or "Hello, I'm Anna and nobody bothers with me because I'm not worth it," (This was Anna's), "Hello, I'm Philip and who the heck am I that anyone would want to listen to me." (This was Philip's.) Say this to each other over and over till you're all rolling round the floor laughing – once you get it out of your head, through your mouth and into a public space, the stupidity of that which has kept you trapped will be so obvious and ludicrous. And, once you realise the silliness of it, you're free.

4. Share with your mirror and release
Alternatively, say your favourite talk talk phrase to yourself in the mirror, over and over for five minutes or more, noticing your inner feelings change from uncertainty to hilarity.

5. In your journal

Each day this week, observe and write down the different talk talk conversations that go on in your head. Just take dictation, not changing or judging whatever it says to you. You will have a main one but there will be others speaking to you. Also, notice when these conversations occur – are they at particular times, with particular people or when you have to do particular tasks? Many are linked to certain events, situations and people.

What's your favourite conversation? Observe your thoughts each day, during this week and notice how you react to things. How do you react when people give you compliments or gifts? How do you feel when someone says they want to talk to you? What does your inner voice say when things go wrong ... and right?

What's your favourite avoidance technique? What do you do to avoid doing the things you know you should?

Now share these with some friends and experience some freedom ... what's stopping you from doing that? It's not your favourite technique or conversation is it? You're not talk talking again are you?

Week Three

Purpose: valuing yourself.

DS – "The world will not be the same without me"

This week's statement will become clear when you read this week's reading. As before, say this to yourself morning and evening and as often as you can or need in between, for each day this week. This week's daily statement is especially helpful when you start feeling low, when someone annoys or belittles you or you start feeling insignificant and ineffectual in the world.

WT – How Would The World Be Without Me?

What lies behind us and what lies ahead of us are tiny matters compared to what lives within us. ~ Ralph Waldo Emerson

A Course In Miracles tells us that God would be lonely if you were not here – every one of us is missed. The world would be a very different place if you were not in it … if you had not been in it.

Let's see just how different the world would be now if you had not been born.

Quietly and sincerely, look at the world about you. Consider how different it would be if you had not been born.

Examples
This may be difficult to do so we'll give you some examples from course participants:

Jonathan couldn't recall anything for some time and then he suddenly exclaimed, in the middle of someone else's recollection, that he'd saved someone's life – a friend and he were swimming at the beach and his friend was being dragged out by the tide. No one else noticed but Jonathan did and so he dived in and dragged his friend back to shore. They were both six years old and he had registered it as a short but exciting moment. If his friend had died, his family, friends, teachers and everyone else around him would have had very different lives. Then, in later years, his friend's wife would not have met him and his two children would not have been born. And Jonathan's wife would not have met him and their son would not have been born. All the people he worked for and socialized with would have had different lives – the list of those affected is endless.

Judith recalled how she, a mother with toddlers, had banded together with a group of other mothers to press the local council to build a play-centre in their neighbourhood. Through that experience she met a lot of people who would have had very different lives if she had not embarked on the project. And the hundreds of children, who formed friendships at the play-centre, would not have met their friends. Just from one project, the world around Judith would have been very different for hundreds of people.

Geoffrey had been a small bore rifle enthusiast and had won many trophies. He started counting the people he had met through the sport, over twenty years and gave up! He realised that the list of people who would have had different lives had he not been there was endless.

Of course, not all of us has saved a life, helped set up a play-centre or been in a club! However, whatever you've done, big or small, has had an effect on the planet and on other people – even if you haven't met up with them. Everyone you email or text would have a slightly different experience of life if you had not communicated with them.

Every one of us has parents – how would your parents' lives have been different if you had not been born? And your siblings, your school friends, your teachers, your neighbours ... the list goes on.

Exercise – A World Without Me

100 Accomplishments
List 100 things that you've done/accomplished that are valuable to you. Not things that others have done – just you. Does that sound daunting? Just start the list and you'll be surprised at how much you've done, once the list gets underway – start writing, now!

Events
From the above list, choose the ten most significant events, for you. Beside each one, list the people involved at the time and the people who would have been involved later on, from the event.

Describe to yourself how you impacted the people at each event and how you made a difference at each event. Again, this takes great courage and honesty to acknowledge that you are significant in the people and events of the world.

People
Start by listing all the people you've engaged with over the years, down a left-hand column. Yes, this could be a very long list! Now, beside every person, write a few words about how you think you made these people feel – happy, alive, sad, informed, silly, loyal, strong, surprised and so on.

It is just not possible to have no effect on the people you meet, whether for a reason, a season or a lifetime. If you're really brave and honest, you know that everyone you've interacted with has benefited from your presence on this earth – you're not here for nothing!

Sharing and feedback
This might seem to be scary … and it is! From the people you've mentioned in your journal (above), pick five and ask them, over the course of this week, how you've affected their lives and what you've given to them in terms of physical, financial, emotional, and/or spiritual help.

You might prefer to email some of them as it seems to be a safer way. However, just remember that it's easier to get miscommunication with the written word – look at how the Bible has been interpreted in hundreds of different ways – and so you'll actually get a clearer and more positive answer from face-to-face discussions.

Also, be prepared to be asked the same question from the person you're talking to – about how they've made a difference in your life.

The Body Shop once had a slogan: *if you think you're too small to make a difference, try sleeping with a mosquito!* If you can make an impact on so many people and so many events, without really trying, think how much of an impact you can make if you really "get your ducks in line", if you:

- Become really clear about who you are,
- Become really clear and focused about why you're really here, and
- Clear all the blocks to being all you can be ... we'll be so proud to have such a person as you doing this course!

Week Four

Purpose: creating a better life.

DS – *"Every day, in every way, I'm getting better and better"*

The French pharmacist, turned psychologist, Emile Coue, coined this affirmation and he found that his patients, saying this first thing each day (and during each day), often had great cures. It has worked for hundreds of thousands of people for over a hundred years and it's your turn to benefit, now!

WT – *Thought, Word And Deed*

It is the nature of thought to find its way into action. ~ Christian Nevell Bovee.

Example
Sandy was moaning that she couldn't find a house for her and her children to rent. We asked her what she wanted.

"Oh, I don't know, a house," she said.

"What sort of house?"

"I don't know, one for me and the kids," she said.

"Can you be more specific?"

"Stop pestering me, just a blooming house is what I want!" she said.

"One, two or three bedrooms?" we asked.

"Oh, three, of course!"

"A garage or a carport?" we asked.

"Oh, gosh, a garage would be better."

We gave her pen and paper and told her to start writing a list – three bedrooms and a garage.

"Why?" she asked.

"Just do it," we said.

"But what's the point?" she asked.

"Just do it," we said masterfully.

We kept pushing her to keep writing down the list of things she wanted in her new house. She was resistant till about item ten when she became excited and couldn't be stopped. She eventually wrote a list of twenty things she wanted in her new home. Six days later she rang to say she had found a house and it had nineteen of the things on her list. The one thing it didn't have was a tree for her son to climb in. The next day she rang to say she'd discovered that there was a park over the road with several climable trees!

Most people aim for nothing and hit it with amazing accuracy! Ask anyone and the chances are that they won't know why they're here (in this life) and what they want out of it. Lily Tomlin said, "I always wanted to be somebody but I should have been more specific."

Ask Richard Branson, founder of the Virgin Group, why he carries a note-book in his pocket at all times. He writes all his thoughts down and he lives a huge life. It works for him. Why not you?

If it's so simple, why doesn't everybody do this? We all want a better life, a life filled with joy and peace, a life that makes a difference, but most choose not to have it. One reason is that it's so simple. We all want the deep therapy, the complicated steps to heaven and most imagine that it could not be so easy. My, how religions have prospered from our need for complication and the rules of others. So why don't you create your own rules?

When we make plans, we have to set goals. And when we set goals, we have the possibility of "failing". And when we "fail", we will be judged by the harshest of judges – ourselves. So, rather than risking the censure of our inner judge, we choose a life less-lived, a life that others set for us, for their judgement is so much softer than our own self-beater.

So, the simple solution to a better life is these 3 simple steps

– Imagination, Expression, Action – the first 3 vowels. If not today, then when?

Exercise – Reviewing Previous Plans and Results

Day One ...

Get out your trusty journal and start writing a list. This is a list of the lists. Write a list of every plan and grand design you've ever made ... and didn't do.

Businesses you wanted to have,
Jobs you wanted to have,
Health & Fitness plans,
Relationships you planned to have,
Houses and locations you wanted to live in,
Educational aspirations,
Hobbies/interests you wanted to pursue,
Things you planned to say to certain people,
Addictions you planned to release from your life,
Behaviours and attitudes you wanted to change, and so on.

Choose the five most important plans from above, and list beside each one how much you did towards them, under each heading – Imagining, Expressing and Actioning.

Imagining

- How thoroughly did you imagine the whole plan or project?
- How much detail, from start to finish, did you think through?
- Did you imagine actually doing it, with all the colours, smells, sounds, tastes and emotions of actually doing it?
- Did you think through all the problems you might encounter and how you would deal with each one?
- Did you decide what you'd do when you had a problem – who to talk to, what other actions to take?
- Did you imagine or think through all the possible outcomes to your life if you succeeded?

Expressing

- Did you write the whole project down, from start to finish?
- Who did you tell – just a few friends or did you reach out to

leaders and mentors who could give you tangible help?
- Did you start a scrap book, diary, spreadsheet, word document or data base?
- Did you paint pictures, cut out magazine articles/images, make sculptures/models or anything else in three dimensions?

Actioning
- What did you actually do towards any of the above imagined or expressed plans?
- Did you do any investigation on the internet?
- Did you approach anyone for help and/or advice?
- Did you spend any money on the project?
- Did you physically create anything?
- Did you make any change in your lifestyle, to accommodate the new plan?

The reason for this exercise will become clear in Weeks Five and Six.

Week Five

Purpose: learn to recover.

DS – "This too will pass"

Considering everything that's happened in this world – ice ages, atomic showers, wars, nuclear explosions, genocide, epidemics – it's a wonder that the earth is still here ... but it is! Whatever drama and/or hardship you've encountered, you're still here. As you remember the worst of times, recall how it felt to be in the middle of that. It seemed, at the time, that nothing would go right, that you were doomed to failure. And yet, here you are, having mastered your life and ready to master the rest of it. Whatever you've encountered, you're still here, you're still breathing, you have the intelligence and the eyes to read this, you have the courage to do this course and you'll go on!

Whatever it is that besets us, passes. Every bit of it. Never forget that.

Then, when you have a breakdown, say this Daily Statement (this too will pass) and recall in vivid emotional and sensual detail what having your goal feels like. Then practice the 5 steps below.

WT – Breakdowns And Breakthroughs

It is time for us all to stand and cheer for the doer, the achiever - the one who recognises the challenge and does something about it.
~ Vincent Lombardi

You're a world-class sprinter, training for the Olympics, and you sprain your ankle. When do you do that? Do you do it while you're sitting on your couch, watching television or while you're out on the track training? Silly question. Of course you'll be more than likely sprain your ankle while you're training, while you're trying to achieve your goal.

In the same way, when does your car break down? While it's sitting in the garage or while you're out driving it? Again, silly question. It usually breaks down while you're driving somewhere.

Most people give up before their goal, before achieving a breakthrough, as they have a breakdown. They think that when something goes wrong, it's a sign that they're doing the wrong thing, and so they stop, just before their breakthrough.

If the Olympic sprinter has a "breakdown", a sprained ankle, what will they usually do? Yes, they get up, hobble to the changing room and then off to their physiotherapist to get the ankle working better. They'll do exercises for it, have more therapy and eventually, when it's mended, return to the track for more training.

If your car breaks down, do you throw it away and stop driving for the rest of your life? Of course not! You get a mechanic (an expert) to repair it. Then you continue driving till you get to your destination.

So, when a breakdown occurs in our lives, why do so many of us throw our dreams away and stop living fully? Instead of getting an expert to help us out, we give up and do something else, while our dream continues to nag us. And bitterness and a sense of failure set in.

The news of the day is that a breakdown is not proof that you're doing something wrong.

- A breakdown is proof that you're on your way to a breakthrough; you're almost there!
- A breakdown means that you're off your couch, out of your garage, and going for it.

If you have seen *The Secret,* you might be wondering why life has taken on a sinister, sad or frustrating turn, since you have been setting bold, new goals and taking action towards them. You think, from the DVD or the book, that all you have to do is to create goals, imagine your future and do something about it … and it all just happens, POOF, just like that. The secret of *The Secret* – the bit they didn't tell you about - is that there's a middle-step on your way to those goals and *A Course In Miracles* tell us what it is:

In the search for anything – love, freedom, peace, abundance, etc – the first thing that happens is that the blocks to them will come up.

If you're searching for love, you'll first be shown all the blocks you have to love and some quite unloving things will happen. Relationships may become very uncomfortable and, when they do, it's your opportunity to recognise and release your blocks to love. If you cannot truly love yourself then others cannot. If you can't believe that you're deserving of amazing love, then you won't be. There are so many ways that we stop love coming to us, by our beliefs, attitudes and actions. And, if love still eludes you, there is probably something you're thinking that is blocking it.

If you set out to make a lot of money, you may, firstly, lose some. This is your opportunity to realise the blocks you have to gaining wealth and to those who have it. You cannot be wealthy while you hate wealthy people. You cannot become wealthy while you feel there is something wrong with having wealth. Recognise your blocks to wealth, release them and you're on your way. And, if wealth still eludes you, there are further blocks to wealth to deal with.

So, when you have a breakdown, you now know that you're close to your intended breakthrough, to your dream coming true.

What do you do with a breakdown? Five things:
1. Realise that you've had a breakdown – it's something you've HAD and not something you ARE. Acknowledge it fully and objectively.
2. Review the breakdown, objectively, and it will reveal what breakthrough it's connected to.
3. Thank the breakdown for the insight it offers and do something about it. Like the athlete and your car, you may need an "expert" to help you through the breakdown. This expert may be a friend, a professional or anyone who can see your situation more objectively and honestly than you can. This is where ruthlessly honest friends are particularly valuable!

4. Return to your vision, restate your goal and revitalize yourself – e.g. get out of frustration and return to knowing that you're on your way to a breakthrough.
5. Do something, anything! Nothing activates help from the universe more than your own action. If you sit and ponder, so will the universe. Obviously, doing something towards your goal is the best thing to do. Activate yourself and you reactivate your goal's achievement.

Exercises – Recreating Breakthroughs

Day One

In your journal, on the first day this week, start writing down the times when you had a breakdown – go back to your notes from the exercise in Week Four. This is any time when you felt that your life had gone wrong, there had been frustrations to your ambitions and dreams, or the flow of life had unaccountably been lost, somehow. Beside each of these unpleasant, frustrating or upsetting events, write down:
- How you felt,
- What you did, and
- What the result was.

It could look like:
- Event 1 – when I tried to … this happened …
- How I felt – frustrated, lost, confused, angry …
- What I did – I shouted at … I curled up … I had a talk to … I stopped functioning …
- The result – I stopped trying to … several other things went wrong, like ... I lost the friendship of ...

Rest of the week …

Review and Undo

During the rest of the week, as you remember further frustrations and breakdowns, add them to this list. Particularly notice the similarities in your feelings, actions and results – we tend to react to things in set ways and, as you know, this course is over 84 days to undo those unhelpful ways and to bring in more functional actions and feelings into your life.

The 5 Recovery Steps
Thirdly, as you experience breakdowns during the week, go back to the above skills you've just learned, do the five steps and notice:
How you feel, and
What the result is.

Write this in your journal as a proud moment of success!

Week Six

Purpose: get a perspective on feelings and thoughts.

DS – "Feelings are not facts. I will go by what I know, not by how I feel."

The *Grow 12-Week Program*, which helps people gain better mental health, has the above as one of their sayings. No matter what your feelings are, they will probably be telling you a lie. Most of the time, your feelings are dictated by your past, what others tell you, what the media tells you and what you tell yourself about your possible future. None of this need be true or factual.

So, as usual, take five minutes for yourself, morning and evening, and say this in the quiet of your still and knowing mind. Then, during the day when anything upsets (or promises to upset you) say the above statement to yourself, remind yourself of the facts and work from them.

WT – It's Only A Feeling

Difficult times have helped me to understand better than before, how infinitely rich and beautiful life is in every way, and that so many things that one goes worrying about are of no importance whatsoever.

~ Isak Dinesen

Example

Philip worked with Kevin at Kilwell Sports Ltd in Rotorua, New Zealand, in the 1980's. Kevin was a pleasant young man, a little unsure of himself and extremely fit – he had a rigorous regime of diet and fitness and never smoked or drank alcohol. One spring morning he skipped into work, full of the joys of life and his boss, Trevor, asked him how he was.

"I'm feeling great," said Kevin.

"Are you sure?" asked Trevor, feeling a bit mischievous "You look a bit peeky – are you sure you're OK?"

"Yea, I'm sure," said Kevin. "I'm feeling really good." Kevin didn't see Trevor winking to Terry, the office manager.

"Morning Kevin," said Terry. "You're not looking too good – did you have a hard night out last night?"

"No, I had an early night," said Kevin, "and I feel good."

Just then Russell approached, sensed the game and asked Kevin, "You feeling OK, mate? Your eyes have blackness around them – are you coming down with something?"

"No ... no, of course I'm OK," said Kevin, "a bit fuzzy in the head but nothing really."

Two more of Kevin's colleagues questioned his state of health and Kevin soon needed to go to the bathroom to see what he looked like in the mirror – he was starting to feel unwell. By morning tea he was feeling horrible and asked Trevor if he could go home to recover.

Kevin came to work the next morning and Trevor confessed that he had been a bit naughty in suggesting that he'd looked terrible the previous morning, when he hadn't at all. Kevin learned two valuable lessons:

How easily we can let circumstances dictate our feelings, and

How powerfully those feelings can affect our body and health.

Now, imagine that you're at your horrible and stressful job and you've planned your perfect, dream holiday for a month's time. While you're working away, you feel stressed, angry, frustrated, overwhelmed and all sorts of other feelings you normally feel at this job. Then, when you think of your holiday, you feel happy, lighter and relaxed ... and yet you're still at your horrible and stressful work. Then, as the holiday approaches, you have more and more uplifting feelings, almost as if you're already there in your paradise … and yet you're still at your horrible and stressful work!

The following week, during the first week of your wonderful two-week holiday, you really relax into it, enjoying every moment of being away from your horrible, stressful work and in this perfect place. Then, near the end of the two weeks, you start to think of going home to work again and you begin to feel stressed again … and yet you're still on your perfect, dream holiday!

Our feelings are dictated by the direction of our thoughts. If we're thinking of a wonderful future, we'll feel great. If we suddenly switch our thoughts to something in the past that we feel guilty about, we'll immediately feel horrible. Then a friend can come in and ask us out for lunch at our favourite café at the seaside and we're quickly happy again. If we wake up feeling miserable and then meet up with someone who tells us how good we look, we'll immediately perk up. Or we might wake feeling fully refreshed and alive and then we pull the curtains and find it's raining and so we immediately switch to feeling miserable … even though the rain's outside and we're in our warm, dry house … inside!

Our feelings are totally unrelated to the reality of our health and our environment. Since we spend most of our time being somewhere where we're not – in our past or our future – our feelings are usually related to where we're not. If we're able to stay in the present, this very NOW right now, we'll have feelings that are more related to what's actually happening with us. And yet, even if we can stay totally present to the now, we'll still be dragging feelings from our past.

For example, if you were brought up in a loving, affectionate home, you will probably enjoy a hug. However, if you were brought up in an abusive and unsafe home, that same hug, today, could feel threatening to you. Same hug, different feelings, based on our different pasts.

Or we might be leaping out of our skin over our latest business idea – we're just so excited about it. Then, the next day, we have another idea that we're excited about and the previous day's one now seems dull and boring. We do this with relationships, jobs, places to live, holiday ideas and every other thing we're involved in – things are amazing one minute and they're dull and boring the next.

And yet, we're told to trust our gut feelings, to listen to our intuition! If our feelings are so unreliable, so disloyal to us, why should we trust them?

1. Doing is knowing
The first answer to why we should trust them is answered in weeks one to four:
1. Clear out your clutter and stand alone with your own thoughts, not those of others, as in weeks one and two, and
2. Create some goals and start actually doing something towards them, as in week four.

We can become excited about a goal but when we have to take physical and tangible steps towards it, our feelings will change. Janet had always dreamed of importing Andalusian horses into New Zealand, from Spain. So, during this course, her "homework" was to research the possibility of doing so. She had to contact the NZ Agricultural Department, the Quarantine Station, the Horse Breeders' Association, the Department of Trade and Industry and numerous other government departments, which meant a very frustrating week, being hung up on, transferred to people who knew nothing and refused to help, finding that different departments had different (and, sometimes, contradictory) rules. Anyone else would have given up but not Janet – the more she had to dig and delve and investigate, the more she loved it. In the doing of it – which is so different from the dreaming of it – she became even more enthusiastic ... and now she's doing it!

Other people, of course, have had the opposite reaction – the dream sounds nice but the actuality, the fact, is not so nice. The doing of will tell you if it's real, for you, or not. If you did nothing, don't be surprised if nothing's happening for you. However, if you took steps towards your goal and found you didn't like where you were going, you've learned something you would never know by just thinking about it.

2. Finding the peace
The second answer is that the only real feeling is the feeling of peace. And, like the Voice for God, peace always speaks second

and always speaks quietly – but it does always speak, one way or another.

So, let's say you're thinking of starting a business and you wake up with this amazing idea – so exciting! As usual, your ego will shout out in excitement and, before, that's what you would have listened to. However, now, you'll listen to that quiet, other, second voice – yes, it feels exciting, but does it also feel peaceful? If there is no feeling of overwhelming peace, you know that the feeling of excitement will soon fade and die. However, if there is a feeling of deep peace, the feeling of high excitement may fade, but the desire to run that business will continue unabated, despite the many other, transient excitements along the way. Once the "honeymoon" is over – for a relationship, a new house, a new job, a new business, a new holiday, a new idea or anything else new – the only thing you can rely on is that deep peace. All other feelings come and go. All other feelings are disloyal to your true mission here. All other feelings are totally unrelated to the actual facts.

Deep peace is that which abides when all the shouting and excitement dies down. Deep peace is loyal to the facts and to you. Obviously, for the small treats, the little impulse purchases, there is no real harm. However, for the bigger and more important decisions in your life, look not for the excitement and the buzz, but for that deep and abiding peace that quietly lingers the morning after … the week after … the year after.

If only emptiness resides after the excitement has died down, then you know to let the idea go. That deep and abiding peace is full and rich – the opposite is empty. If the feeling of peace does not quietly abide under the rampant ego feelings, then move on to where peace abides. That is the feeling that is real and that is the feeling to follow.

Exercises – Finding Facts And Deep Peace

1. Fluctuating feelings
Go back to your thoughts of Week Four, when you were taking steps towards your failed goals – write down in your journal the thoughts you had as you took each step.

Did the "rightness" of it increase or decrease?

Did the excitement of the project rise and fall, wax and wane?

Did you, at any time, feel that "rightness" or that deep and abiding peace. When did you feel it?

Was the rising and falling excitement influenced by things not related to your project – the weather, your friends, your job, future anticipations, past fears, media announcements ...

2. Catching the feelings

Now, make a quiet moment for yourself and review one of the times you initially felt excited and then quickly switched to disenchantment – it might be Week Four's exercise or any other time when you were about to embark on something major for you.

You started out feeling confident, that it was the right thing to do, and then your feelings changed ... though the facts remained the same. What was it that got your mind to change?

Was it other people, the media or something that happened outside your mind?

Was it something that happened in your mind – did you recall last time you attempted something like this? Did your talk talk set you back again?

Write the reasons for your change of feelings, whatever it was.

3. Catching the peace

Recall other times when you've sensed that great peace – yes, you have at some time in your life. It may have been about doing this course, about saying "thank you" to someone who does a good deed, about helping someone, about not doing something you ought to have, about doing something you were told not to, about doing something that scared you – things big and small.

In the quiet of your mind, ask for those decisions and events to be brought forward. As each one comes up, feel the deep peace that they bring, that abiding peace that cannot be shaken by transient events and uninformed opinions.

Write those decisions and events down ... in big, bold letters so you can see them from across the room. These are decisions and events that should be big and bold in your life!

Week Seven

Purpose: understanding anger and depression.

DS - "I am never upset for the reasons I think"

Again, this is from *A Course In Miracles* and serves to remind us that no matter what we feel is wrong, that's not the actual cause. If we're upset with someone, it's not them who is at fault, but what they mirror in us – aspects of ourselves that we see in them.

As you'll discover below, all negative feelings come from the one core feeling, which is our sense of disconnection with God, Love, The Source or whatever you want to call "it".

So, use this for 3-5 minutes, morning and evening and at any other time you feel upset, angry, niggled or depressed for any reason. As you repeat this, the real cause of your distress will become known and, as it's in you, you'll then be able to deal with it – you can't "fix" anyone else but you can "fix" yourself!

WT – Anger And Depression

Anger will never disappear so long as thoughts of resentment are cherished in the mind. Anger will disappear just as soon as thoughts of resentment are forgotten. ~ Buddha

Anger and depression are the same thing. They look different but they come from the same source. They are two common (and opposite) ways of expressing emotions – they are not, however, the emotions themselves.

A mechanic will not say, "Your car is noisy". He will say, "Your car is noisy because there's a hole in your muffler" (or whatever the reason). The source of the problem is not the noise but it's from something mechanically wrong with your car.

In the same way, the source of the problem is not anger and/or depression but from something emotionally/spiritually wrong in your soul. There's an emptiness that won't go away. Both anger and depression are the result of perceiving unmet expectations.

Does it help for someone to tell you that you're suffering from depression or anger? What can you do with that information? Nothing! What you really need to know is what the deeper problem is, not its outer manifestation.

Ponder this:

When you act angrily, what causes that action? You're feeling lost, let down, disappointed, picked on, criticised, useless, without direction, lonely, insignificant or some other negative feeling?

When you act depressively, what causes that action? You're feeling lost, let down, disappointed, picked on, criticised, useless, without direction, lonely, insignificant or some other negative feeling?

Aha! So they come from the same source and you just choose a different reaction to those negative experiences. Some people explode outward (anger) and some implode inward (depression). Some people do both.

The anger and depression are the tip of the iceberg, and all those feelings are hidden underneath, unseen.

Any of the emotions "under the water" of the iceberg can trigger anger or depression – the choice of reaction is yours, depending on your upbringing, nature and state at that moment. Whether you choose depression, anger or one of the many behaviours in between those two, is up to you. In general, men are forbidden to cry so they'll choose anger, while women are forbidden to be angry so they'll choose depression.

Anger does not happen to you – you choose it as your outlet for your emotions. Depression does not happen to you – you choose it as your outlet for your emotions.

Go beyond your behaviour to the emotions and you'll better understand your actions. So, how do you stop being depressed or angry?

Reconnecting with your source - atonement

If your angry or depressive behaviour comes from negative emotions, where do those negative emotions come from? Even the most angry or depressive person has "good days" - times when they're not behaving angrily or depressively. So the triggers to that behaviour aren't always there. Where do they go on "good days"?

Despite the reservations that some people have about the Bible stories, The Fall (as per Adam and Eve) is in every religion, in some way or another. The basic idea of The Fall, from whatever religion you choose, is that we were once connected to God and we felt that connection in every moment – were at-one with God, The Source, Love or whatever you want to call that which is bigger than all of us. Then came The Fall which is a time when we chose to become separate from God and to do things our way, for whatever reason. Ever since then, we have been missing our direct and constant connection with God and we've been trying to get it back.

You may be able to recall a time when you were in some sort of team, club, business or relationship and things were going beautifully. You were winning, you all got on well and you all had a strong feeling of connection with each other and with the aims of the group.

Then something happened and that connection stopped. You stopped winning, the business started losing money, the relationship became uncomfortable or whatever. Then the "blame game" started - or maybe it started before your fall - and, instead of supporting each other, you started picking at each other and finding fault with each other. That feeling of connection died and you all felt a greater separation from each other.

The Fall was like that. We were connected, something happened and we became separated. Since then, we've striven to become one again – to become at-one … to atone.

Every single thing we do is either:
1. An act of love, or
2. A call for love.

We all want to return to Love, or connection with God, and everything is related to that. When we don't feel that connection, the negative feelings creep or blunder in and we react – using a variety of behaviours, anger and depression being the two most common.

So that's where anger and depression come from:
1. we feel a loss of connection, then
2. we feel bad, and then
3. we react to that.

Where does that take us?
When we act angrily or depressively, people around us want to really connect with us and be closer, don't they? No? Of course not! Our behaviour pushes people further away, increasing the separation and worsening the original problem!

So we need to do something different if we want a different result. What can we do?

Exercises – Recovering the Connection

No cheating
Rather than saying you're angry or depressed, say you're feeling lost, worried, abandoned, embarrassed or any of the other feeling words that you're feeling. Take anger and depression out of your vocabulary and substitute doing words with feeling words.

You might want to cheat - instead of saying anger you'll use words like mad, wild, furious, pissed off and so on. Instead of saying depression, you'll say feeling down, moody, listless etc.

Those are all "surface" words, words to describe your behaviour. With honesty, we'll look below the surface and seek out words to describe that which caused our reactions - words like belittled, shamed, embarrassed, lost, abandoned, not listened to, ignored, humiliated, picked on, disappointed, worthless, useless and so on.

Using a substitute for anger or depression gets you where the labels got you in the first place – nowhere! The idea is to honestly identify why you're feeling the way you do so that you can move forward, not backwards again. Onward and upwards, we say!

Observing Depression

So, now that you're ready not to cheat, create a quiet and uninterrupted space and time, with your journal and your thoughts (and a pen/pencil) and recall an upsetting incident which put you into a depressive state.

1. Briefly describe the incident in your journal,
2. List the feeling words that were rising as the incident happened, and
3. Ask, in the quiet of your mind, what was it that triggered your feeling of separation. Write that down.

You were feeling OK some time before the incident and then something happened to disturb that OK feeling – what was it?

Observing Anger

Recall an incident which put you into an angry state and do the above four steps.

Listening to the lion

Anger can roar like a lion. Rather than being afraid of it, listen – it has a message from that deeper, wiser part of your being. Get a baby-sitter, get someone to mind the shop and take yourself off to your coach, counsellor, friend or journal and let the anger roar. Just let it all out, undiluted by judgement or fear. Much of the noise will be meaningless but there will also be information for you – information on what needs to change and how. Listen and take notes or get your friend to take notes. Re-reading them later, you will be amazed at the depth of wisdom from that old lion!

Posture Awareness

Anthony Robbins says that people don't get depressed, they do depression. In a depressed state, we frown, put our lower lip out, look down, hunch our shoulders, bend forward, take short, shallow breaths, let our arms flop and point our toes inward – closing in. When you're feeling good, take the above stance and see how you feel. Depressed?

Next time you feel depression coming, take on an opposite stance – open your body, relax your face, look up, smile, straighten your shoulders, stand up, take deep breaths, raise your arms and straighten your feet.

If anger is your favourite reactive state then you'll have to frown, tighten your jaw, glare, lean forward, take short, shallow breaths, clench your fists, raise your shoulders, tighten your stomach and stand with your legs firmly apart. When you're feeling happy, take on this stance and see how you feel. Angry?

Now, do the opposite – relax your face, smile, breathe deeply, open your hands, relax your shoulders, raise your chest gently, stand upright and bring your legs closer together. Practise it and next time you're in a tense situation, slip into this "cool" stance and watch your positive new self deal with the situation in a completely different (and better) way.

These techniques may not get to the bottom of the problem but they do help to change your state to one that is open to returning to the source of the problem and dealing with it.

Week Eight

Purpose: letting go of guilt and regret.

DS – "Let miracles replace all grievances"

Start your morning in quietness while repeating this saying to yourself. Choose a person who is causing you to feel regret or guilt. Already a person has sprung into your mind and it may not be the one you're expecting. Whoever it is, think about them and why they are causing you to feel pain in any way. Spell out to yourself all the ways and reasons they're causing you annoyance, disappointment, pain, fear, sadness, anger or whatever way they're upsetting you.

A Course in Miracles tells us that there are no levels of difficulty in miracles – anything can be overcome. Some people are able to forgive the murder of a loved one and others cannot let go of annoyance of someone losing a shoe lace. The size of the problem is never the problem. The problem is always our refusal to let the problem go. Besides, no matter how long and hard you choose to let someone else control your life, theirs still goes on regardless – you're the one with the problem, not them! As they say, if you're harbouring a grievance, you're allowing someone to live in your mind rent-free.

So, having listed all the ways this person has aggrieved you, change your mind about them. Choose to see the inner person, the spirit-self that Jesus or Buddha might see. They are not a bad person; they just acted in a way that did not meet your expectations. Choose to see the goodness within them and know that all it takes is a little willingness from you to lose the chains that bind you.

Do this exercise every morning, choosing a different person each time. Also, you may like to do it every time someone upsets you during the week – it's like taking a refreshing shower, washing the dirt of grievances off.

WT – Regret And Guilt

Some luck lies in not getting what you thought you wanted but getting what you have, which, once you have got it, you may be smart enough to see is what you would have wanted had you known.
~ Garrison Keillor

Both regret and guilt are cut from the same cloth and both have an equal ability to stifle your life force. If either of them are running around in your mind, you're being kept back from the magnificence that you truly are. And yet, if they're used in the right way, they can direct you to make the right decisions to create a more powerful and fulfilling life.

If you ask any older person what they regret in life, you can be sure that the things they regret are not always the things they did – they regret the things they didn't do. And yet most of us spend an inordinate amount of energy trying to decide whether we should do this, that or the next thing. How will you feel when ...

- The book you write does not sell millions,
- The person you confess your love to does not reciprocate,
- The job you apply for does not happen,
- The gift you buy is not fully appreciated,
- The effort you put in is not rewarded.

If you do those things and they don't work out as planned – as long as it was done from love (not from fear) and didn't harm anyone – you may feel sad. You can also feel proud that you did them from your heart-felt desire. However, if you don't do those things, you'll only ever feel regret, not knowing if you should have taken the courageous step you wanted to.

You see, most of us have *aughtism* which is a whole catalogue of the things we ought to do in every circumstance. The information we used when we published our life-catalogues was gained from our upbringing, social environment, cultural/religious background, peers, employers, advertisers and many other people we'll never meet. What most of us have forgotten to do is update our Aughtism Catalogues. We hold ourselves back from what we'd love to do because clause 53.a.II of our particular catalogue says we ought not to do this because that's what it says.

You probably know the story of the newly-wed husband who asked his wife why she chopped the tail and neck off the turkey before roasting it. She didn't know but said that's what her mother always did. He asked her mother who didn't know but said that's what her mother always did. He asked his wife's grandmother why she did it and the old lady said it was because the turkey was too large for the oven! Since then, turkeys have become smaller and ovens have become bigger and yet we still do it because … well, because that's what others do!

Yes, we should have waited for an adult before we crossed the road when we were two – but we've now grown up. Yes, women didn't ask men out 200 years ago but we're now in the 21st century. No, men weren't nurses 100 years ago but that was 100 years ago!

Like regret, guilt can roar at us and we jump. We agree to do things for others when we'd rather not – we feel guilty saying "No".

If you're thinking "I shouldn't have done that" or "that shouldn't have happened" you're locked in a battle with yourself and you cannot win. If you're blaming your parents, your own stupidity, your culture, your circumstances or anything else, you're using regret unproductively.

What your parents did was what they did. What you did is what you did. What others did is what others did. Everyone will agree that it happened and harping on about it will not convince them to agree any more. No denying it happened. Today is today and it's not yesterday. Psychologists tell us that around 85% of families are dysfunctional. Everyone had something bad happen to them – abuse, loss, sadness, pain, fear, uncertainty. It's time to let the past go and choose not to let it (and the people in it) control our lives today

Martha Beck says that you're finished grieving when you see someone gaining what you regret losing and you feel joy for them. You may even feel joy for the lesson you learned from your loss. Till that time, however, you haven't finished grieving – you're still stuck in regret or guilt. And, if you're still stuck there, you're going nowhere useful.

Let's say you've been trying to have your brilliant manuscript published and, to date, you've been turned down by every publisher you've tried. How do you feel when you hear of an aspiring writer who has had their manuscript accepted by a publishing company? If you feel annoyance, unfairness, anger or depression, you're still stuck in regret or guilt. However, if you feel really happy for them, you're probably over it.

Let's help to get you out of stuck and into unstuck.

People are often unreasonable, irrational, and self-centred. Forgive them anyway.
If you are kind, people may accuse you of selfish, ulterior motives. Be kind anyway.
If you are successful, you will win some unfaithful friends and some genuine enemies. Succeed anyway.
If you are honest and sincere people may deceive you. Be honest and sincere anyway.
What you spend years creating, others could destroy overnight. Create anyway.
If you find serenity and happiness, some may be jealous. Be happy anyway.
The good you do today, will often be forgotten. Do good anyway.
Give the best you have, and it will never be enough. Give your best anyway.
In the final analysis, it is between you and God. It was never between you and them anyway.

~ Mother Teresa

Exercise – Dipping Under the Waves of Regret and Guilt

1. Admit it
If you don't feel joy for others gaining what you've lost (or haven't gained), admit that you're not over it. Write down in your journal, "Yes, I'm not over that time (name the situation) and I'm still mad/sad about it. I admit it and I want to get out of it." You will feel some relief from admitting it and saying that you admit it – on this rock we stand.

The easiest way to become unstuck from anything is to, firstly, admit where you are – you're in breakdown, on to a breakthrough. The breakthrough will not happen unless you admit to the breakdown.

The second thing is that being clear about where you're at – rather than pretending you're where you're not – is that clarity happens. Just the admission, itself, may show you a way out.

2. Get grieving

After admitting to your regret or guilt, get on and do some grieving – talk about it with a coach, counselor, friend or your journal. Read books on grieving, Google internet articles on grieving, revisit the site of event that's giving you madness or sadness.

You might feel it's right to discuss the event with people who were involved – this is a time to be discerning as this is your issue, not theirs. Everyone is doing their best with what they know, in every given moment, just like you. You've got more social and emotional skills now, than you had then and hindsight has given you much more clarity – they may have learned nothing in the meantime. So, it's not a time to confront people and expect apologies and/or reparations – your badgering them about will not educate them in the way you've been educated. Your job here is to get clarity and peace for yourself. So, the approach is that you're looking for facts and not trying to change or accuse anyone – you're bigger than that.

So, get some impartial and honest advice before revisiting the "enemy" in your war on guilt or regret. Or, go on to the next exercise which will help with both the grieving and clarity, about what to do next to restore your power.

3. Get underneath the guilt and/or regret

The sweeping tide of grief will be flowing over a beach of golden sand. Put your hands beneath the water to discover the gold ... gosh, that was poetic, wasn't it! Of the four basic emotions – sad, mad, glad, and scared – grief and regret will contain either or both of the first two. In this exercise, simply complete and repeat the sentence: "I am sad that ..." or "I am mad that ..."

Write in your journal why you're sad and/or mad – speak out

and write down every reason why you're full of regret or guilt. Just keep going till you run out of reasons to be sad or mad.

4. Recalling the breakthrough

Like that exercise in Week 5, we know that we wouldn't be having a breakdown unless we were on our way to a breakthrough. Recall the time that you're feeling the guilt or regret around – what was it you were aiming for then?

Another way to look at it is to look at what's missing. Look at the many reasons you feel sad or mad (from 2. above) and then list, in your journal, what's missing that, if it were present, would make the sad and/or mad disappear. Your *what's missing* could be more than one ingredient and is/are most likely the same as what you were aiming at before the breakdown. If the thing/event that caused your guilt/regret had not happened, what would you have that you don't have now? Start your list and keep writing till you've exhausted all possibilities, like:

Health	Friends
Relationships	Jobs
Feelings	Money/wealth
Opportunities	

5. Bringing the past back

Now, with your *what's missing* firmly in mind, take a quiet moment to close your eyes and imagine your life with all that abundance and freedom (or whatever your what's missing is) in it now. Savour the feelings and the things you would be doing. Imagine your life with your what's missing in it and imagine what jobs, people, activities, holidays, awards, assets and other things you would be enjoying now. Once you've had a mindful of that amazing experience, write it all down as:

I am working at …

I am living happily with …

I am now feeling …

I am going on holiday to …

And so on. Now thank your guilt/regret for giving you the insight into what you really, really want and decide, today, which of those above experiences or feelings you're going to start doing something about … something every day this week.

Week Nine

Purpose: to see the past differently.

DS - *"I can choose to see this differently."*

This statement, from *A Course in Miracles*, helps to remind us that what we think anything means – an event, a comment, a look – is a story we create. Facts do not control our feelings (per week seven) – stories and perceptions about those facts do. So, every time we feel upset, it is because we have chosen a story we don't like … and we can, in an instant, change that story into a different one.

So, take five minutes, morning and evening, to pamper your mind with the knowledge that any feelings are not based on fact and that anything we feel is up to us to take charge of and turn to our benefit. We are the authors of our stories and the masters of our lives.

WT – *Events And Stories*

Someone may have stolen your dream when it was young and fresh and you were innocent. Anger is natural. Grief is appropriate. Healing is mandatory. Restoration is possible. ~ Jane Rubietta

The events in our lives are not what shape our lives. These events simply happen to us. They do not make us what we are. Most of us think that what happened to us is what makes us the way we are today. Whether our parents were abusive or supportive, whether our teachers were empowering or nasty, whether our neighbourhood was poor or affluent, whether our skin was black or white, whether our bodies are male or female, whether our friends are law-abiding or criminals, whether our health is good or bad – all of these factual things are seen as the life-shaping elements in us. You may have believed that it would be difficult to change yourself for those events and circumstances will not change – they were in the past and the colour of your skin, nature of your parents and every other thing you currently have cannot be changed. By believing these unchangeable and historical facts have made you as you are, you may well feel that you cannot be any other than that which you already are. Sorry, but you're wrong! You can change.

You can change who you are and that change will be much easier when you realise that the events in your life have nothing to do with your feelings, behaviour, status, assets and relationships. What has actually shaped your life are the stories you have created around the events in your life. Let us explain:

Examples
At the beginning of 2002 Philip met Mnumbeko Mpongo, a 27 year-old black woman, from Cape Town, who was speaking at the same international AIDS conference he was. She had contracted HIV by being gang-raped by six men, three years previously. From that horrific experience, she could have made up some entirely logical stories:

- The world is unsafe
- Men are not to be trusted
- The innocent and undeserving get the worst
- I'm going to die … and all sorts of other stories.

However, she eventually chose to make up a different story from that incident. After being frightened, angry and disempowered, initially, she chose to change her attitude, with the help of Dianne Lang, an AIDS worker. When Philip met Mnumbeko, she had no ill feelings towards her attackers. In fact, her stories were:

I am going to live through this HIV. She's now in an unprotected sexual relationship with a man who also has HIV and both of them are recovering - their CDC counts are coming down each month.

I am thankful for those rapists. She says that she was destined to become yet another illiterate, unemployed black girl and that incident turned that around. Because of it, she's now an AIDS educator in prisons and for the council.

I have learned just how powerful, intelligent and creative I am and that I can make a real difference in the world.

In her passionate and moving speech she said that she didn't need our sympathy or our acceptance for she had come to respect and accept herself, no matter what the outside world threw at her or thought of her.

The important thing here is that the story she created has shaped her life. If she had chosen any of the first stories (the more negative ones) her life would have been very different. Her story about the event is what has her living a full and productive life. The event has no effect at all – it was just a catalyst for her to create a story … any story.

Once upon a time there was a boy called John whose greatest lesson in life was that he was not good enough. One day he rushed home from school and excitedly told his mother about how he had come top of his class in a French test and he had got 98%. His mother's only comment was, "So what did you do wrong with the 2%?" His perception was that whatever he did, it was never good enough and he came to expect condemnation for everything he did.

This boy became Philip's father.

The way he perceives it, he was the little golden boy until he was seven – up to that age he could do nothing wrong and his sister could do nothing right. Then, for no apparent reason, his mother reversed the system and, from seven onwards, he could do nothing right and his sister could do nothing wrong. The important point here is that Philip's father perceived his childhood to be very unhappy, while his sister (2 years younger) sees her childhood as very happy. It doesn't matter what our parents (and other people) actually do; it is what we perceive they do that shapes our attitudes and behaviour.

You may know children from the same family who have grown up with quite different attitudes and achievements. One of them may feel completely blessed with their wonderful parents, friends, teachers and others in their life, while the other sees the same people in their life as being abusive, obstructive and disempowering. They've lived near-identical events in their childhood but the stories they've created around those events have drawn them to very different destinies.

What happened to you was neither good nor bad. The 'good' or 'bad' was your interpretation, or perception, of what happened. So, the stories you tell of your life will not be the events themselves, but your perception of the events. However, you can change the stories and recreate your past, opening yourself up to greater possibilities. And, as you separate your stories from your events, you can take away the judgements and analyses you've had of those things. Freeing yourself from judgements of others also frees you from the judgements you have of yourself. And, in that freedom, you can stand outside yourself, as the silent witness to your life, seeing every event as simply an event, unhindered by judgements, and as an opportunity for growth and greater self-awareness.

So, let's start unravelling the stories and getting clear about the events in your life:

Exercises – Recreating Your Stories

1. By yourself
In your journal (or page 87), write down the main events of your life – the ones you remember and the ones that you feel were life-changing or life-defining. Beside each event, write down the story you have created around each event, ensuring that you include all the judgemental and emotional words you feel about each event. Then simply rewrite the story into a positive, uplifting and/or inspiring one.

2. With a friend
There are several different ways of doing this exercise but the simplest is this:

If you're upset by someone or over an event of any kind, you can have a friend take you through this, even if they're the reason you're upset. There are three steps.
   1. They ask you what the event (not the story) is that you're upset about – you tell them.

2. They then ask you what your feelings are around that upsetting event – you tell them.
3. They ask you when the first time was that you felt those identical feelings – you tell them.

This event will probably be in early childhood and you may have forgotten it, till you're asked about it. As it comes to mind, describe the event and then separate out, from the event, the story(s) you've made around that story.

The above three steps have more impact if you write down what you tell your friend – you're moving from imagination to expression. Also, you'll have it in your journal for later review.

Understanding brings appreciation and appreciation brings love.

What you will probably discover is that this story has dogged you for most of your life:

If you felt that your father abandoned you, you have probably felt, ever after, that other men or authority figures have abandoned you.

If you felt, in that (above) incident, that your mother criticised you unfairly, you have probably felt that other women or authority figures have criticised you unfairly.

As you unravel this story around that first event – no matter how small or how well-remembered it was – you'll realise that you've been carrying the proof (of abandonment, criticism or whatever it was) ever since in most of the more unpleasant events in your life.

As you recall that incident and the story around it, you will be able to free yourself from the story and to stay with the event, the fact and, as you now know, we can never be upset by a fact – we can only ever be upset by a story or perception we weave around a fact.

Obviously, the facts won't change but your story can – try doing the exercise again, now, with a different (more positive) story, and see how you feel about what happened. In a way, you're changing your past, which will free your future.

The last step is, obviously, to thank your friend for helping you release the huge burden you've been carrying all your life, quite unnecessarily.

Event 1 ....
....
....
....

Original Story 1 ....
....
....
....
....

Reconstructed story 1 ....
....
....
....
....
....

Event 2 ....
....
....
....
....
....

Original Story 2 ....
....
....
....
....
....

Reconstructed story 2 ....
....
....
....
....
....

Week Ten

Purpose: to learn that we create our lives.

DS - "I am being the change I wish to see."

This is a slightly altered quote from Mahatma Gandhi and it mirrors the way the universe works. Rather than looking for the world to change to our desires – a process that never works – we decide how we'd like our world to look and then become that. From your stance and attitude will flow all that you desire.

So, morning and evening and every time in between – especially those times that we feel aggrieved about something or someone – we'll remind ourselves with the above statement and become a little more like the way we'd like the rest of the world to be. If we feel people are being ungenerous, we will become more generous. If we feel that people are judgemental, we'll become less judgemental. Focusing on ourselves means that we're focusing on what it's possible to change.

WT – It's All Smoke And Mirrors. Well, Mirrors Anyway

What you are comes to you. ~ Ralph Waldo Emerson

You may not like to hear this bit but here goes. Whatever is happening to you, right now, is what you've attracted to yourself. Ouch! Did that hurt? Whatever is happening in your life, at this minute, is the accumulation of the thoughts, dreams, prejudices, fears and loving thoughts you've had in the past, up to now.

Do you know anyone who is always late? And they always say, "Oh, I'm always late." Their belief in themselves – that they're always late – creates circumstances that just happen to make them always late.

Do you know anyone who is continually lucky? And what do they say about themselves? "Yes, I just seem to be a lucky person!" What they believe about themselves brings the universe to align them with luck.

So, whether you're:
rich or poor,
happy or sad,
lonely or with friends,
sick or healthy …

Whatever situation it is that you find yourself in is a result of how you've thought about yourself in the past. … and how you're thinking about yourself right now.

Of course, you haven't been shouting down the street, "I want to be poor!" or "I just love being sick!" or "I just love feeling lonely!" No, you have not said that … we presume!

Your current situation is a perfect mirror of your thinking to date. Did you get that? … to date. And the significance of that to date? Simply that you can change your thinking and any new situation will be the result of your changed thoughts.

Caroline Myss talks about woundology, a word she invented – it refers to the fact that people with a certain wound (a negative belief about life) will attract someone who has a similar wound:

Someone who has been abused and feels that people are unsafe, will attract a partner who abuses them.

Someone who feels that it's impossible to make enough money will attract someone who is unable to make enough money.

Someone who thinks that sickness is difficult to avoid will attract a partner who is often sick.

Right now, we'll get you to dispassionately observe your current situation. What you cannot measure you cannot control. What you will not measure you cannot change. This is not an exercise in self-flagellation. It's simply an honest look at where you are in terms of health, finances, relationships/marriage, friendships, motivation and sense of direction and hope.

Exercise – Looking Into It

1. Who are you?
Write down a list of the six people you most constantly connect with, on a daily basis. If you have children, count them as one person. Write your list and, beside each person's name, write down the emotional and attitudinal attributes that each one radiates to you - happiness, sickness, positivity, support, negativity, grumpiness, silliness, seriousness and so on.

Those attributes are your future! Are they the ones you'd choose from the catalogue of life?

2. Who do you want to be?
Write down a list of the attributes, abilities and types of people you feel would help your journey. You're obviously not going to toss all your old friends out but you are going to focus on what kind of "new blood" you'd like to inject into your system.

3. What is your life going to look like?
Start by writing in your journal all the things you want in your life. Draw pictures, diagrams, lists, stories … anything that best explains what your perfect life will look like.

Now, over the following week, find yourself a large piece of paper (at least A3-sized), a white-board, a cork-board or a large surface that you can pin/glue things to. On this surface, start collecting pictures from magazines that epitomize your life from now on –

- Places you'd like to travel to, from travel magazines,
- Clothing that speaks of your new station in life,
- People who you admire and wish to emulate,
- Assets (cars, houses, boats, musical instruments etc) you wish to have.

Think of what you want in your life and then go searching for an image that depicts that – keep adding to your vision board and keep it in a prominent place in your home, so you see it often.

Week Eleven

Purpose: finding your place in the world.

DS – "All gifts I give others are my own."

From *A Course in Miracles*, this (slightly altered) saying reminds us that giving and receiving are the same. The more we give to others, the more we receive ourselves. The more we value and express our greatest talents and attributes, the more everyone benefits.

The converse is also true – the more we hold ourselves back and hesitate to become the best we can be, the less we can give to others … and the less we receive ourselves.

WT – What Keeps You Going?

The best way to find yourself is to lose yourself in the service of others. ~ Mahatma Gandhi

We (Anna and Philip) love all aspects of personal development – teaching, learning, writing, doing – and we've both had that passion for a very long time. However, there were times when we were writing this course – which also necessitated creating a website, advertisements, promotional work, working with lots of other people and fitting our personal life in between it all – when we felt overwhelmed and tired of it. What got us back on track was to remember why we were doing this – to enable millions of people to make a positive difference in their lives in a way that they could afford, both in time and money. When we forgot our tired little bones and remembered that we were doing something for our planet and the people on it, something we were passionate about, all that tiredness went. You and the millions of other people who are benefiting from this course, and the other resources on our website, are what kept us going.

We all have down times – sad, mad and bad times – and what keeps us going through the hardest of times is keeping others in mind.

Victor Frankl was a German/Jewish psychologist during WWI and he was sent to Auschwitz concentration camp. As he went into that dreadful place, he set himself three missions:

To survive,

To learn something about himself, and

To take what he had learned to help people when he got out.

What he learned was that peoples' survival in that camp depended on how much hope they held for the future and what hope they had for making a difference.

One man was going to commit suicide and Viktor reminded him of his three children who would have no father at the end of the war if he did that. The man took his children as his reason to live and he survived.

Another man was also going to commit suicide when Viktor reminded him that his important scientific experiments would not be completed if he died, robbing mankind of that important work. The man decided to survive the horrors of the camp and lived to complete his scientific research.

Another significant moment came for Viktor while on a predawn march to work laying railroad tracks. Another prisoner wondered out loud about the fate of their wives. The young doctor, Frankl, began to think about his own wife, and realised that she was present within him.

The salvation of man is through love and in love. I understood how a man who has nothing left in this world still may know bliss, be it only for a brief moment, in the contemplation of his beloved.

~ Viktor Frankl

Up to now, this course has been about you, what you've gone

through and what you want from life. All of it is an empty shell if there is no desire to serve.

We've all experienced the thrill of thinking that something we don't have is better ... and then realising it's not so good when we get it:
- We long to live in a more exotic part of the world and, when we do, we find all sorts of things wrong with it.
- We long for a better partner/spouse and when we get her/him, they're not much better than our previous one, once the honeymoon is over.
- We plot and plan for that amazing job that someone else has and, when we eventually get it, it's much more stressful than we imagined.
- We think that beautiful house on the hill, by the lake or in the woods will be the answer to our prayers. Yet, when we start to live in it, we find that the plumbing is bad and so are the neighbours.

Whatever we're looking for to complete our lives will do no more than provide is with a "honeymoon" period, till the shine of it wears off ... unless the reason we're looking for it is beyond ourselves. If we want to help others as well as to improve ourselves, in some way, then the resulting accomplishment of that goal will hold lasting value and fulfilment.

What's your mission?

This is the BIG QUESTION most of us have asked ourselves. And, strangely, most of us have no answer for it ... well, we think we don't! The other strange things is that, as Neale Donald Walshe says, there is no large blackboard in the sky with the words "Anna Bradbury's mission is to ..." or "Barak Obama's mission is to ..." There are two schools of thought:

1. That we have a specific mission that we're here to fulfil. Until we do that, we're going to be unhappy and unfulfilled, and

2. That we have no particular mission at all. We're here to learn certain things and there are a thousand different ways and situations in which we can learn these particular things.

It's unlikely that we'll ever know the answer while we're alive so we've just got to guess what it's all about. And, whether there's some mysterious mission or not, it's all a bit pointless if we aren't told what it is. We suspect that God/The Universe is not that unfair as to give us a mission we'll never know about so we assume, from that, what we've got to give is that which we most love giving. For some it's cooking. For others it's saving the Amazon forests. Some love politics, some sport, some business and others art. Some love being a parent, some a business executive and others an Olympic swimmer. Whatever you love doing is probably your mission, given our lack of information to the contrary!

Since we weren't given our life's instructions at birth – or at any other time – we're going to presume that what you love doing is what you're here for. So, within what you love doing, how can you make a difference in the lives of others? By now, you've found quite a few things you'd REALLY love doing. Let's keep it simple and stick to those.

Anna loves creating from ideas, personal development and making a difference. Philip loves writing, teaching and personal development and so this course arose.

Jamie Oliver loves cooking and so is making a difference in the diets of British people.

Engelbert Humpledink loves singing and so uplifts us with his beautiful voice.

There is no talent that cannot be used for good, in some way. So, how are you going to benefit the planet and its people, while providing you with peace, joy and fulfilment?

Not knowing what you don't know

Now, imagine two circles, one inside the other. In the inner circle are all the things you know that you know – how to tie your shoe-laces, speak English, drive a car, bake a cake, sing a song and so on.

Outside this inner circle, but inside the outer one, are all the things you know that you don't know – how to make a million dollars a day, speak Slovenian, sing like Pavarotti, do heart surgery and so on. Most of our lives are spent trying to expand this inner circle or, in other words, focusing on what we know that we don't know and trying to make it known by study and practice.

However, very few people look outside the second circle to the rest of the universe where are kept all the things you don't know that you don't know. In stepping into this void we step into nothingness, absolute potential and possibility.

In focusing on what we have or know, we are only looking inside the innermost circle and, occasionally, stretching the sides a little as we add to what we've got or know. Also, if we simply start from where we are and try to fix the bits that don't work, we'll simply stretch our inner circle a little. For example, if we start with "I'm too fat" and then try to lose weight, it usually won't work. The fact is that everyone, absolutely everyone, knows how to lose weight – eat less and exercise more – but they don't all do it. They don't do it because they're starting from the inner circle and trying to work outwards. Most people want to have more money in the bank and don't have it, despite the fact that they do know how to do it – simply spend less.

However, if we go beyond ourselves (our current talents and assets), being open to the possibility that there are infinite possibilities we know nothing about, what could we find? With the focus of fulfilling a need, we may have no idea of how to do that but, if we open ourselves up to the simple possibility of meeting or achieving it, the world of undreamed-of possibilities will come to our door and it will take us to places, feelings and experiences we never imagined could exist.

In the above two examples (less weight and more money) we could simply go to the outer circle, to the empty bowl of life, and create the possibility of a body we're proud of or the possibility of complete abundance, realising that those states could come to us in ways we could never imagine.

So how do you access this area of the universe we call the place where you don't know what you don't know? One way is to simply forget who you are, forget what you know, forget what you have and take an imaginary flight around the world and beyond the world. Then, in your mind, you can look back and you'll be drawn to one particular area of pain. Now, simply say to yourself, "I stand for the possibility of that pain (whatever it is) being healed". Then go back to your ordinary life and (if you really meant what you said) watch it become extraordinary in ways you never thought possible. In reading this you have accidentally tripped over the line of your outer circle and fallen into the void of that which you didn't know what you didn't know. You see, you didn't know that you didn't know how to find this place (you never knew it was here to know about) and here you are in it! Not only that – you now know that you know where you are and how to get back home to your knowing space. And, as you arrive back home, you are bringing with you the knowing of how to access your void, your place of unlimited possibilities, your place of talents you never knew, any time you choose.

Now, watch your life unfold in its miraculous way and, please, tell us about it, for your experience will inspire others and the more that others are inspired, the more possibilities are able to be opened up for you and us. On this rock we stand – it works for us and it will work for you too.

Exercise – What Are You Really Here For?

A picture of you.

You may want to go back to Week Four's exercise to help here.

Get yourself a HUGE piece of blank paper (as big as you can) and

Get some coloured felt pens, pencils or crayons.

In the centre, draw a picture of yourself and stick figures are fine if you're not an artist.

Use one side of the paper for your past and one side for your dreams.

On the past side, write down all the things you've done that have any meaning for you and feel free to use different colours, pictures, frames and anything else that adds to this picture of you.

On the other (dream) side write down everything you've ever dreamed of doing and haven't done yet. Again, make this as interesting, colourful or funny as you can.

Now, with different coloured felts/crayons/pencils, draw lines between activities/interests that are similar or where you can see a connection between them. Obviously, with everything on this HUGE piece of paper, these lines are unlikely to be straight ones!

This, then, is a picture of the "has been you" and the "could be you". Sit back and look at the picture and you may start to see recurring themes and you may even see connections between things you've done and dreams you've had – connections you may not have recognised before. They may not be identical but they could be similar.

Journal time
In your journal, now, write down the ideas, interests or themes that occur the most, from this marvellous picture of yourself. Write these themes in order of frequency – those occurring the most frequently, write at the top of your list.

From this you will begin to get a picture of what you really do love and what you're actually here for. It's a lovely part of the universal plan that what we most love is what we're here for and what we're best at. A confusing part of the universal plan is that what we most love may not seem, at first glance, to be something we can make money from and exist on.

The story is told of a young man whose greatest loves were dressing up and eating in restaurants – obviously he could not see how to make money out of that. However, with some brainstorming by himself and with a group of friends, he created a business of it. He now approaches restaurants that are empty and offers to eat at them – people are usually reluctant to eat in empty restaurants. So, he takes a partner along for a meal and, as passers-by see the happy couple enjoying a meal, they come in. This young man gets a commission on each new customer who comes in while he's there and he makes a good living from it.

So, having identified something that recurs in your life and which gives you the greatest joy, start playing with ideas of making it work. If you're having trouble thinking of something by yourself, ask some friends for their help.

Week Twelve

Purpose: getting what you really want.

DS - "Nothing is for nothing, everything counts. Does this action take me towards or away from my goal?"

If you don't already have a goal, you'll have one by the end of this week! Whatever that goal is, there is no "sitting on the fence". Whatever you do will take you towards it or away from it. So, as you consider every little or large task during the week, ask yourself if that task will take you towards or away from that goal, knowing that nothing is for nothing and everything counts – every decision, thought, word and action (even the decision not to act) has an effect either way.

WT – Acting As If

Success is often the result of taking a misstep in the right direction.
~ Al Bernstein

Walk along any street and you soon work out who the wealthy people are and who the poor people are. Not only their clothes – the wealthy usually walk with more confidence, heads up, looking ahead, sometimes smiling and looking like they've really got somewhere to go. The poor usually seem uncertain of themselves, have heads down, look down, look unhappy and shuffle along as if they have nowhere in particular to go.

The poor usually spend more of their money on food that's not good for them, and can be seen at McDonalds, KFC and Burger King. The wealthy usually eat better food at home and are seen out at better restaurants.

The poor seem to gather around betting shops while the wealthy don't take such chances with their wealth. Happy people look different from sad people – you can immediately see it. Friendly people look different from unfriendly people. Shy people wear sunglasses when the sun's not out – confident people don't need them.

Teenage boys and girls try to bolster up their lack of confidence by acting as if they're tough.

We all know, from birth, that there's a set of behaviours and a dress code for every different station in life. So, the obvious thing would be to decide which station we want to move to, emulate those who are already there, and have it happen. Well, that seems a bit weird but it works better than you might think.

Example - acting *as if*

Mike Dooley is an author, speaker – and a few other things – from Florida, USA, who also appeared in *The Secret* DVD. His favourite saying is "Thoughts become things – choose the good ones!" One of his favourite ways of manifesting things is acting *as if*. He talked about a particular conversation he had with one of his course participants. She was living alone, ready for a relationship but could not attract anyone. Mike suggested that, instead of parking her car in the middle of her garage, setting one place at dinner and sleeping in the middle of her bed – acting as if she was alone – that she park her car to one side, set two places at her table and sleep on one side of her bed – acting as if she had a partner.

She was a little dubious but decided to try it. And it worked! Four weeks later she met her new and amazing man and just over six weeks later he was parking his car to one side of her garage, enjoying her cooking and sleeping on one side of her bed.

Mike uses the acting as if technique for himself too. At one time he really, really wanted a motor boat but knew it would take over two years to be able to afford it, given his current cash balance and income. So he started acting as if he did have the money and was actually going to buy a boat – he checked boats, prices and specifications on the internet and in magazines, he visited boat yards, inspected boats, talked to friends and boat experts about them and generally immersed himself in boats, boats and more boats.

Then, six months later, he realised that he had the money to buy a boat! Somehow, his income had expanded to meet his deepest desire, which is what really amuses him about it now – by the time he had the money to buy a boat, he'd gone off the idea of buying a boat! However, he was thankful for the expansion in his income and for the benevolence of the universe.

So, what is it that you really, really, really want? Let's find out with this exercise … then we'll get you doing it. Sound simple? And why should any of this be difficult?

Beware of SAD Bags!

Before you start, remember that you have a little bag (some bags are bigger than others) on your back – a bag you've been carrying since early childhood. The bag is called your SAD bag. Since you heard your first promise, you've been disappointed many, many times. You wanted a pretty doll or a green racing car for your fourth birthday and all you got was a silly hat! You wanted to go somewhere on holiday but your parents couldn't afford it. You wanted to sit next to that hunky guy but your teacher wouldn't let you. You wanted to go to a dance with that beautiful girl but her parents wouldn't let her. You wanted that promotion but the boss's favourite got it. You wanted to have a happy family and all you've got is a divorce and two confused children. All your life you've ordered something from Universal Takeaways and they've always delivered something a little less – they've short-changed you all along. And that is where sadness comes from – you have an expectation and it isn't met. In fact, you've had so many unmet expectations, you've learned to ask for a little (or a lot) less than you really want. You've deliberately short-changed yourself in your desires so that you won't be disappointed, for disappointment hurts. Disappointment (or getting less) hurts more than expecting less – or does it? The SAD (Systems for Avoiding Disappointment) bag is getting very heavy with all your unrealised dreams filling it up. Before you start this exercise, please take the bag off, put it outside, open it up and let the undreamed dreams out. If you want to put the bag back on later, you're welcome, but if you leave it out for a day or two, it will dissolve. Your choice ... Now, let's do the exercise:

Exercise – You're Already There

Day One

This exercise usually takes 40-60 minutes so ensure that you have physical and mental space for at least that long. It's fine to do it with other people but do not look at what each other is writing. This is a very private exercise and even if it's your spouse, you do not ever have to share it with them if you don't want to ... and they don't need to share what they've written with you. After you've finished writing the ten categories down, and making your choice, you may then feel comfortable with sharing part or all with someone else. Only do this if you feel totally comfortable doing that. These are the ground rules you must all set before starting. So, let's go.

In your journal, write your name and date at the top except that the year is not this year, but the year three years from now. If today is 5 April 2019, write 5 April 2022. You have now transported yourself three years into the future. You awake on the morning of 5 April 2022 (or whatever your date is) and what you discover is that ...

Write down in your journal, under the following headings, what you want your life to be like and, remember, no SAD bags – dream and imagine the most bountiful and fulfilling life you can.

Surrounding environment. Close your eyes and imagine that you're waking up in your absolutely perfect place. As you wake up and look out your window, in your mind with eyes still closed, what are you surrounded by? Is it trees, a desert, the sea, a cave, a busy city etc? Is it sunny, snowing, rainy, warm, dry etc? Is it quiet or can you hear people, music, birds or traffic? Which country is it? Close your eyes, dream and what do you experience? Now, write it all down.

Personal energy. As you open your eyes and stretch, how do you feel? Are you calm, excited, peaceful, inspired, loving, centred or whatever. Write down all the feelings you'd like to have, each day.

Surrounding people. As you wake up, who is beside you (a loving partner, no one, the cat …) and who else is in your abode – children, parents, grandparents, friends. Dream up the ideal number and type of people you'd like to live with.

Assets. As you look around on this beautiful new day, you think of the main assets you have – house(s), car(s), business, investments etc. List them and, beside each, write the freehold value of each of them – no loans or mortgages exist in this perfect world! Also list any special assets you'd like – ones that don't necessarily have great monetary value but have high emotional value for you.

Income. As you sit down to a delicious breakfast, you open an envelope that shows your income for the last year – write down the amount. Just remember that there are people currently earning over a million dollars a day so there's no need to limit yourself – nothing is impossible. Also, this income comes in steadily, week after week, whether you're working or not.

Holiday time. While munching on your breakfast, with your favourite people and creatures about you, you smile as you think of the number of weeks a year you have to spend as you wish. Remember that your work is something you're passionate about so you'll want to spend some time working! Also, if you only want four weeks a year, you may as well stay in your current job.

Pastimes. During this (now longer) time that you have for yourself (and considering your huge income that's not dependent on you being there to earn it) there is no limit to the things you can do to amuse, inspire and expand yourself. In three year's time, what can you see yourself doing? Perhaps it's travelling, workshops, bungee jumping, having time for your family and friends, having time for yourself, writing your best-seller or being pampered in some way. Write down the things you would like to be doing and be very specific about this. Don't just write travel. Write travel and then write down why you're going, who you'd like to meet, what you'd like to see and what you want to bring back from the experience. Most importantly, be specific about what your pastimes will give you and how they will improve, amuse or enlighten you, rather than what you do in them.

Addictions. As you relax into this perfect day, you reflect on the addictions you've freed yourself of. These may be the obvious things like cigarettes, alcohol or drugs or they may be something else you cannot possibly live without. These may be things like your business, your cell-phone, other people being happy, other people liking you or your friends, drama or stress. You don't have to do without any of these things – you just don't want to need them.

Worldly gifts. You came here for a purpose and, as you know, this will probably not be known in its entirety yet. However, in this moment, write down what contribution you would like to make to create a better world. On paper, you can become the World Ruler, save all the forests, eliminate poverty, cure your mother's cancer, be a perfect mother and restore the Leaning Tower of Pisa, all at once. We're not being practical here, just imaginative. Have fun!

Worldly receipts. What will you receive for achieving one or more of your (above) goals? If you do save the forests or eliminate poverty, what will be the benefits to you in terms of physical, emotional and spiritual gains? Write down the feelings and other gains as you imagine your great work completed.

You may need to continually remind yourself to take off your SAD bag again for, mysteriously, you may find it's returned. Write down what you'd like and, each time ask yourself, "Is this what I'd really, really like?" Cross out what you've written and put down your true desires. You will know what you really want but you could be afraid to ask for it. For example, you may write $100,000 income – think again and be real with your desires. You may change that to $500,000 then to $1,000,000 and then to $50,000,000 – keep going till you feel a sense of peace and rightness with what you have written.

Now, 2 more steps:
Look down the list and tick the three categories that jump out at you, saying, "Pick me, pick me!" These are the three most obvious

things you want to start working on.

Next, look at the three things you've just ticked and choose one – the most urgent thing you feel you need to work on or improve in your life.

Over the next week ...

... you will commit to doing something about working on that one chosen category. Obviously, you will not be able to be a millionaire in a week but you can start researching business ideas, training and educational opportunities, get books from the library, talk to financial experts ... there are all sorts of things you can do to start on whatever it is.

If it's about relationships, it's unlikely you'll be married to your soul-mate in a week! However, you can talk to friends about ideas, join clubs, read books on relationships, call someone who is special and ask them out for a coffee, think about joining Toastmasters to help with your confidence, start getting fit ... there are so many things you can think of to start the ball rolling.

It's like a train – it takes a lot of energy to get it moving, it takes off slowly but once it gets up steam and speed, it's hard to stop it. The hardest part is starting to determine to do it this week. If not now, then when?

Go back to the *Imagining, Expressing and Action* exercise in **Week Four** and apply those questions to your chosen categories.

A New Beginning

Now you've finished the course, you need to:
1. Raise your right hand in the air,
2. Drop your hand down so it lays on the back of your right shoulder, and
3. Pat yourself on the back for completing this course.

You've shown courage and persistence – among a lot of other great attributes – and you need to acknowledge yourself for this.

Having completed this course with a little willingness, a lot of diligence (and a little "forgetfulness" at times) you will have noticed the world around you changing. There are still wars, arguments, anger, despair and judgement out there but, somehow, they're happening less in your mind and less in your life. This journey has not always been easy and there's always a temptation to go back to your old ways, the ways that didn't work but at least were familiar. Some of your old friends, activities and habits will be calling you back but, despite the awkward feelings you have about learning a new skill, a new way of thinking, you really can't go back.

You've seen a light, a Truth, a glimmer of sanity and hope. You just can't go back. So, how do you keep moving yourself forward? Simply by surrounding yourself with people and resources that will remind you of the light and sanity that you are; people and resources that will help grow the peace, power and joy you've started to find inside you.

If you're in Britain we suggest you join the *Miracle Network* which acts as a resource organisation for all things related to *A Course in Miracles* in the UK - a free support, contact and information service for 3,500 students of *A Course in Miracles*, mainly in the United Kingdom, although the Network also has members overseas. They produce a bi-monthly magazine, run monthly Miracle Café meetings in London, put on workshops and seminars by local and overseas presenters, sell books, CDs, DVDs and other resources. There are over 80 groups that meet regularly in peoples' homes and you can find your nearest group on the website, www.miracles.org, or by phoning the administrator on 08445 670 209.

If you're in USA, there are many groups and two of them are:

The website of *The Foundation for Inner Peace* (http://acim.org/) (FIP), the publishers of *A Course in Miracles*, is based in California. The site provides information about the activities of the FIP, including publications and copyright issues.

The Foundation for A Course in Miracles (http://www.facim.org/) offers a comprehensive website. Located in Temecula, California, the Foundation, run by Gloria Wapnick, is a teaching institute. This site contains a summary of *A Course in Miracles* teachings, information on the books and tapes published by FACIM and articles from their *Lighthouse* newsletter.

There are many other organisations and resources on the Miracle Network site at http://www.miracles.org.uk/links/links.php.

Attitudinal Healing is organisation based on *ACIM* principles and it is run by Gerald Jampolsky and Diane Cirincione. There are over 60 Attitudinal Healing centres throughout the world and Gerald and Diane have written many books between them.

There have been hundreds of books written about *ACIM* and some of the better known ones are *Love Is Letting Go Of Fear* by Gerald G. Jampolsky, *The Disappearance of the Universe* by Gary R. Renard, *A Return to Love* by Marianne Williamson and Ken Wapnick has written dozens of books.

Because there are no limits to our thinking or to our minds, our minds are joined. This means that if you have a need, it will be answered; including the need for others who share your now-found peace and joy. Just ask and they will come.

Letting Go

For a complete explanation of this process by an expert, read the book, *Letting Go* by David Hawkins.

This process is used to let go of negative thoughts you have about someone or about an event. It works for any thought and it works like this:

1. When a negative, annoying or disturbing thought arises in your mind, do not try to ignore it. Instead, become very present with it. You can imagine it sitting in your hand or right in front of you. Whatever you do, just be with it - not hating it, not loving it, just observing it.
2. Now that the thought is there, look at it closely and see what it looks like. What colour is it? What shape is it? What texture is it? What size is it? What feelings does it bring up for you?
3. When you observe the feelings arising from the thought, be with them, as you were with the thought. Just observe them. See where they sit in your body. Try to describe them to yourself. Are they hard? Hot? Slimy? Cold?
4. As you observe the thought and/or feelings, just calmly staying with whatever pain, uneasiness or discomfort they bring up, you will notice that they disappate. This could take some time. However, with practice, it will happen quicker and quicker. Just be with them. Allow them to be their worst, most pervasive and most uncomfortable. Just keep allowing and they will subside.
5. When they have subsided, simply hand them over to God, the universe or whatever you call that which is bigger than

all of us. Let them go to that bigger intelligence. Watch them go and give gratitude for what they have taught you while they stayed with you.

The Sedona Method (https://www.sedona.com/HowItWorks.asp) uses five questions:

Step 1: Focus on an issue that you would like to feel better about, and then allow yourself to feel whatever you are feeling in this moment.

Step 2: Ask yourself one of the following three questions:
- Could I let this feeling go?
- Could I allow this feeling to be here?
- Could I welcome this feeling?

Step 3: No matter which question you started with, ask yourself this simple question: Would I? In other words: Am I willing to let go?

Step 4: Ask yourself this simpler question: When?

Step 5: Repeat the preceding four steps as often as needed until you feel free of that particular feeling.

You will probably find yourself letting go a little more on each step of the process. The results may be quite subtle at first. Very quickly, if you are persistent, the results will get more and more noticeable. You may find that you have layers of feelings about a particular topic. However, what you let go of is gone for good.

About the Authors

Anna

Most of the work I did in my early career was for profit-making organisations, but after experiencing the satisfaction that comes from being an advocate and making life better for others, my passion for helping people was awakened and I chose to only work for organisations dedicated to helping people in some way.

Eventually I joined with Philip in relationship, later marriage, and in creating, producing, editing and writing our own inspirational magazine. After two years, we let this go and moved to the UK to live, work and travel.

When I returned down under, I retrained as a Life Coach and have never looked back! This modality truly embraces everything I am passionate about and it is exceptional in its ability to be a vibrant catalyst for positive change through powerful tools and curious questioning.

Since 2004, A Course In Miracles has been a key foundation in my life that has helped me recognise my wrong-minded thinking and to choose right-mindedness. Through the power of forgiveness I have deep peace in my life (when I choose it that is!).

Philip

I was born very early in my career as a human being and I made the most of the choices available in this outer world. Delving into business, teaching, writing and inspiring people to chase down the best version of themselves took me to many places, friendships and experiences. Then, somewhere along the road, I found the inner world more attractive than the outer one.

Heeding Anna's advice to bloom where I was planted, I began to appreciate the inner growth that comes of stillness, forgiveness .... and found that my outer world expands in proportion to the inner expansion. I should not have been surprised at this!

Anna and I met *A Course in Miracles* and life has never been the same. We owned a publishing business then joined in marriage and now we're on a journey of a lifetime!

Books by Philip J Bradbury

Non-Fiction
Life Rejuvenated
Whose Life Is It Anyway?
The Lawless Way

Some-Fiction
53 SMILES
97 SMILES
Whispers From God
Dactionary – the dictionary with attitude
The Meaning of Larf

Fiction
Circles of Gold
The Last Stand Down
My Whispering Teachers

For more information on these books, see:
Philip's website: www.philipjbradbury.com
Blog: https://pjbradbury.wordpress.com/

Book by Anna Bradbury

Confessions of an Aha! Artist - stories, insights and confessions from life coaching clients ... and other musings
For more information on this book, and Anna's life coaching, see:
Anna's website: http://www.annalouiselifecoaching.com/
Facebook: https://bit.ly/2KOay2k

www.ingramcontent.com/pod-product-compliance
Lightning Source LLC
Chambersburg PA
CBHW070434010526
44118CB00014B/2043